The Bible, Physics, and the Abilities of Fallen Angels: The Alien Abduction Phenomenon

Paradox Brown

The Bible, Physics, and the Abilities of Fallen Angels: The Alien Abduction Phenomenon

Paradox Brown

Copyright © 2009 Paradox Brown

All rights reserved. Fine to print out for personal use, give away, email, etc. but not ok to print for personal monetary gain.

Second Revision Copyright © 2011 Paradox Brown

Pictures, images, and quotes are copyright their respective owners.

This material was first presented as a lecture in 2009 at the First Christian Symposium on Aliens – ChristianSymposium.com.

Supreme thanks to Jesus Christ for helping me write this, and whatever is worthwhile and true in this is dedicated to Him.

Also Many thanks to Joe Jordan, Mike Slack, Jackie Slack, and Guy Malone for their help in the formation of this lecture.

Table of Contents

Preface — 7

Abilities of Fallen Angels as Described in the Bible

Chapter 1 - Visions and Dreams — 11

Chapter 2 - Physical Manifestations, and Physical Interactions during Visions — 21

Chapter 3 - Visions - Time Perception Manipulation, Extreme Realness, and Wide Variety of Possible Content — 29

Chapter 4 - Summary of Visions, and False Visions Caused by Fallen Angels — 37

Analysis of Modern Alien Abduction Experiences

Chapter 5: Alien Abduction Experiences False Visions and Terrifying Dreams — 43

Chapter 6: Alien Abduction Experiences Physical Manifestations — 55

Chapter 7: Alien Abduction Experiences False Visions Combined with Partial Physical Manifestation — 59

Modern Physics and the Abilities of Fallen Angels

Chapter 8: False Visions, Dreams, and Physical Manifestation — 65

Chapter 9: Time Perception Manipulation — 95

Chapter 10: Conclusions — 109

Resources — 127

Preface:

This book is titled "The Bible, Physics, and the Abilities of Fallen Angels". Before we get started, I want to point out that this book is on what I call "fallen angels" and not on what I would call "demons". I make a distinction between the two, as I think there is a hierarchy of evil spirits, and some are more powerful than others.

We see this in scripture:

Eph 6:12 "For we wrestle not against flesh and blood, but against <u>principalities</u>, against <u>powers</u>, against the <u>rulers of the darkness</u> of this world, against <u>spiritual wickedness</u> in high [places]."

Rom 8:38-39 For I am persuaded, that neither death, nor life, nor <u>angels</u>, nor <u>principalities</u>, nor <u>powers</u>, nor things present, nor things to come, Nor height, nor depth, nor any other creature, shall be able to separate us from the love of God, which is in Christ Jesus our Lord.

Evil spirit beings are regularly divided up into types in the Bible. Some types of evil spirits are more powerful than others. I am defining "demons" as the less powerful evil spirits that require gaining influence or control over a person or animal in order to have any physical presence. The evil spirits that Jesus and the disciples cast out of people in New Testament are the only spirits referred to as "demons" biblically.

What about the demonic hierarchy of evil spirits?

I do think that demons can affect dreams, and it is this kind of dream which can sometimes cause one to believe they have experienced an "alien abduction" although there is no physical evidence left from the experience, as is the case in other "alien abduction" accounts. These dreams I would attribute as being caused by evil spirits of the demon level, or sometimes fallen angels as well.

Demons also cause waking oppression. Some contactees and abductees while awake practice channeling of what they call "aliens". This could also be attributed to demons. Finally, demons, once they have a physical influence or control over a person's body, can cause seizures, illnesses, ailments, and madness, as seen in the Bible. Some things related to the "alien abduction" phenomenon may be attributable to demons in this way.

However, besides these few things, there are many other parts of the "alien abduction" experience that simply do not match the physicality level or powers of demons. They would require a higher physicality and power, as fallen angels have.

Dan 10:13 But the prince of the kingdom of Persia withstood me one and twenty days: but, lo, Michael, one of the chief princes, came to help me; and I remained there with the kings of Persia.

And I am defining "fallen angels" as being the more powerful evil spirits that can have a physical presence that is not dependant on inhabiting a person or animal's body. These are more comparable in abilities to Holy angels, or to Satan, having comparable abilities, and of the same or a similar class or as him.

Fallen angels are of the class referred to in Daniel as the "prince of the kingdom of Persia". We read that Gabriel could not overcome the "Prince of Persia" by himself, but needed Michael's assistance. So, in Daniel it is made clear that some spirits are more powerful than others.

The distinction having been made, this book is mainly on fallen angels and not on demons.

However, I do want to make a note. I once asked Joe Jordan, the president of the CE4Research Group (which undoubtedly has worked with more alien abductee cases than any other Christian organization that I can think of, some 500 cases) what abductees typically reported to their research group.
He responded that the vast majority, even over 90% of abductees, usually started out recounting their experiences with, "I've had these dreams..."

And so the research indicates that there is reason to think the vast majority of "alien abduction" experiences have a more dreamlike, and less physically-real-seeming, quality to them. Of course, this leaves less than about 10%, of "alien abduction" experiences in which the abductees have reported a physically-real-seeming quality to the experience. Any thorough explanation of the mechanics of "alien abduction" must of course cover both types of "alien abduction" experiences. What follows attempts to be such an explanation, covering all the many aspects of what has been reported. There perhaps may be more of an emphasis in this study of explanation of the more physically-real-seeming experiences, which is necessary for a thorough explanation. But please do make note that the attention given to experiences with this physically-real-seeming quality in no way negates that this type of experience is reported by the research to be the less common sort of experience.

The Abilities of Fallen Angels as Described in the Bible

Chapter 1 - Visions and Dreams

To better understand what these fallen angels can do, we are going to take a look at the abilities demonstrated by angels in the Bible. Then we will compare the abilities of fallen angels as described in the Bible to modern alien abduction accounts.

It would make sense that the abilities of fallen angels would be the same as the abilities of Holy angels, as God originally made all of them to be Holy angels, who were capable of carrying out certain tasks for God. These tasks include giving messages, through dreams and visions, or delivering a message while appearing as a man. Though they usually remain invisible, angels protect people from harm (Psa 91:11-12). They function as the army of God (Rev 19:19): they destroyed Sodom (Gen 19), brought down the wall of Jericho (Josh 5-6), and smite people (1 Ch 21). God created angels to be able to do things like these.

Angels can do miraculous supernatural things, and unfortunately fallen angels can still do many of these same things, as they were created with these abilities. But they use them for evil and deception. As such we're going to be looking at examples found in the Bible of both Holy angels and fallen angels, to establish what the Bible says are the abilities of angels in general. In this we can have a better idea of what fallen angels can do in general. And also a foundation for better understanding the activities that fallen angels are engaged in today, which seems to include "alien abduction" experiences.

<u>Visions caused by Angels</u>

Angels can cause what the Bible refers to as "Visions".

Dan 10: 1-12 In the third year of Cyrus king of Persia a thing was revealed unto Daniel, whose name was called Belteshazzar; and the thing was true, but the time appointed was long: and he understood the thing, and had understanding of the vision. In

those days I Daniel was mourning three full weeks. I ate no pleasant bread, neither came flesh nor wine in my mouth, neither did I anoint myself at all, till three whole weeks were fulfilled. And in the four and twentieth day of the first month, as I was by the side of the great river, which is Hiddekel; **Then I lifted up mine eyes, and looked, and behold** *a certain man clothed in linen, whose loins were girded with fine gold of Uphaz: His body also was like the beryl, and his face as the appearance of lightning, and his eyes as lamps of fire, and his arms and his feet like in colour to polished brass, and the voice of his words like the voice of a multitude.* And **I Daniel alone saw the vision: for the men that were with me saw not the vision; but a great quaking fell upon them, so that they fled to hide themselves.** Therefore I was left alone, and saw this <u>**great vision**</u>, and there remained no strength in me: for my comeliness was turned in me into corruption, and I retained no strength.
Yet **heard I the voice of his words**: and when I heard the voice of his words, then was I in a deep sleep on my face, and my face toward the ground. And, behold, **an hand touched me,** which set **me upon my knees and upon the palms of my hands**. And he said unto me, O Daniel, a man greatly beloved, understand the words that I speak unto thee, and stand upright: for unto thee am I now sent. And when he had spoken this word unto me, **I stood trembling**. Then said he unto me, Fear not, Daniel: for from the first day that thou didst set thine heart to understand, and to chasten thyself before thy God, thy words were heard, and I am come for thy words.

What can we observe from this passage? Daniel calls what he experienced a "great vision" (Daniel 10:8) which was caused by an angel. While having this vision:

1. It was real to the bodily senses: Daniel was in his body, he saw with his eyes, he heard with his ears, he felt a hand of an angel touch his body, felt being on his hands and knees and later standing up, and he felt bodily trembling

2. The vision Daniel saw was overlaid on top of the reality everyone else could see, but others could not see the vision. (Dan10:7)

3. What Daniel saw was unusual, and even impossible-seeming, such as a face with the "appearance of lightning". Also the voice of the singular being he was seeing sounded like a multitude of voices.

4. Daniel was awake, and not dreaming, nor in a trance.

Daniel's body was still surrounded by objective reality, the river, the landscape, and the men fleeing from something they couldn't see but felt emotionally. The men could see the river and the landscape. However, Daniel's mind was also seeing a vision from an angel overlaid onto this objective reality, and this vision that he interacted with felt completely real to his bodily senses. He saw it, he heard it, and felt it, yet no one around him could even see it, though they felt fear.

The Bible confirms that Visions caused by angels are experienced with the senses, seen with the eyes, heard with the ears, felt tactilely in the body, stating it plainly in Eze 40 and 44.

In the <u>visions</u> of God brought he me into the land of Israel, and <u>set me</u> upon a very high mountain, by which [was] as the frame of a city on the south. And he brought me thither, and, behold, [there was] a man, whose appearance [was] like the appearance of brass, with a line of flax in his hand, and a measuring reed; and he stood in the gate. [angel] And the man said unto me, Son of man,<u> behold with thine eyes, and hear with thine ears,</u> and set thine heart upon all that I shall shew thee; for to the intent that I might shew [them] unto thee [art] thou brought hither: declare all that thou seest to the house of Israel. Eze 40:2-4

Then brought he me the way of the north gate before the house: and I looked, and, behold, the glory of the LORD filled the house of the LORD: and <u>I fell upon my face</u>. And the LORD said unto me, Son of man, mark well, <u>and behold with thine eyes, and hear with thine ears</u> all that I say unto thee concerning all the ordinances of the house of the LORD, and all the laws thereof; and mark well the entering in of the house, with every going forth of the sanctuary. Eze 44:3-4

Before going any further, I think it is important to be able to conceptualize what a Vision is. What would an experience like this be called in the present-day world? If a man today claimed to have seen an angel, which he saw with his eyes, heard with his ears, touched, and who no one else with him could see… There are many today who would say he must have had a "hallucination". Not only that, but also a "visual, audio, and tactile hallucination". And there are many people today who would say such a man should see a psychologist or psychiatrist for help. This would only be more likely if the man started claiming he was a prophet, and writing down his experiences, because he thought these "hallucinations" were important enough that God wanted them recorded to be shared with posterity. Then he might really be labeled as "crazy" and locked away. But this would all be the case only because much of the world today rejects that God exists, that angels exist, and rejects that angels have supernatural abilities and can interact with mankind.

A hallucination is defined as:
"a sensory experience of something that does not exist outside the mind, caused by various physical and mental disorders, or by reaction to certain toxic substances, and usually manifested as visual or auditory images."
-Dictionary.com

"a sensory perception that does not result from an external stimulus and that occurs in the waking state. It can occur in any of the senses and is classified accordingly as auditory, gustatory, olfactory, tactile, or visual. It is a symptom of psychotic behavior, often noted during schizophrenia, as well as of other mental or organic disorders and conditions."
 –Mosby's Medical Dictionary

Inherit in the definition of a "hallucination" is the forgone conclusion that it is "not a result of external stimulus" (like an angel), it "does not exist outside the mind" objectively (like angels or the spiritual side to reality itself), and it is "caused by various physical and mental disorders" and is a "symptom of psychotic behavior".

The difference between a Vision and a hallucination is that a Vision IS a result of external stimulus, namely angels, who are an external stimulus that do exist outside of the mind, and a Vision is not caused by a physical or mental disorder, nor is it a symptom of psychotic behavior.

But like a hallucination, a Vision is a sensory experience, like Daniel is described to have had.
Of course, differentiating between a "hallucination" and a "Vision" is entirely a matter of if one can prove as to whether the sensory experience was caused by an angel or not caused by one. It is hard to prove that a "hallucination" was not caused by external stimulus when that external stimulus could be an angel, who stays invisible and does not declare their presence.
In fact, one could just as easily assume that all "hallucinations" are actually caused by angels (holy or fallen) and are therefore Visions, as one could assume that all Visions are not caused by any external stimuli (but rather from some physical or mental disorder) and are therefore "hallucinations". As to which is which, the deciding factor is all a matter of personal spiritual beliefs, bias, and very subjective personal interpretation of the experience.

But for Christians, the Bible is full of many examples of Visions caused by angels. And Visions in the Bible have quite a bit of variety to them, for instance some happen while awake, and some happen while in a trance state. An example of a Vision had during a trance is in Acts 10:9-17.

On the morrow, as they went on their journey, and drew nigh unto the city, Peter went up upon the housetop to pray about the sixth hour: And he became very hungry, and would have eaten: but while they made ready, he **fell into a** *trance*,
And **saw** *heaven opened, and a certain vessel descending upon him, as it had been a great sheet knit at the four corners, and let down to the earth: Wherein were all manner of fourfooted beasts of the earth, and wild beasts, and creeping things, and fowls of the air.* And **there came a voice to him**, Rise, Peter; kill, and eat. But **Peter said**, Not so, Lord; for I have never eaten any thing that is common or unclean.
And **the voice spake unto him again** the second time, What God

hath cleansed, that call not thou common. This was done thrice: and the vessel was received up again into heaven. Now while Peter doubted in himself what this *vision* **which he had seen** should mean, behold, the men which were sent from Cornelius had made enquiry for Simon's house, and stood before the gate.

Observations on this passage:

1. Peter had this "vision" in a "trance", while awake, and not asleep. The "trance" is not described as "dreaming". It seems likely that those preparing for lunch who were with Peter saw Peter in this trance state. However, this trance state is not described as "dreaming". Peter was awake, and not asleep, though in a trance state.

2. Peter observed being in his body - this is implied by him being able to optionally "rise, kill, and eat". Peter also is seeing with his eyes, and hearing with his ears.

3. Peter, like Daniel, sees unusual or impossible-seeming things.

During this trance Peter experiences what the Bible calls a 'vision' ("horama" Strong's 3705). Earlier in Acts 10:3, Cornelius also receives a "horama" vision, specified to be caused by an angel. Later, in Acts 12, Peter is unsure whether or not he is having another vision, when an angel is present: "Peter followed him (an angel) out of the prison, but he had no idea that what the angel was doing was really happening; he thought he was seeing a vision" Acts 10:9 NIV

These Visions (which communicate a message) are Biblically associated as being caused by angels, as Holy angels are God's messengers; the Greek word aggelos meaning "messenger". Many times angels give messages from God by causing dreams or visions.

The word above in Acts 10 for 'trance' is "ekstasis" (1611 in the Strong's). The second definition is "a throwing of the mind out of its normal state, alienation of mind, whether such as makes a lunatic or that of a man who by some sudden emotion is transported as it were out of himself, so that in this rapt condition, although he is awake, his mind is drawn off from all surrounding objects and wholly fixed on things divine that he sees nothing but the forms and images lying within, and thinks that he perceives with his bodily eyes and ears realities shown him by God."

So, even the Strong's Concordance defines this trance as an experience in the mind, which is perceived with "bodily eyes and ears", or in other words is real to the bodily senses. In Peter's case, he describes that he perceived hearing with his ears, seeing with his eyes, and speaking with his mouth. This indicates he perceived himself as being in his body, experiencing something which seemed real to all the bodily senses. However, it is implied that those around Peter perceived him as being in a trance state. Peter might not have known he had been in a trance, but may have just thought he had been awake, if there had not been other people around that saw him in a trance.

Another instance of a vision, which was also likely facilitated by a Holy angel messenger (Se Rev 1, 1:1) happened to Paul and the men with him in Acts 9 (related again in Acts 22).

Acts 9:3-8
And as he journeyed, he came near Damascus: and suddenly there shined round about him a light from heaven: And he fell to the earth, and heard a voice saying unto him, Saul, Saul, why persecutest thou me? And he said, Who art thou, Lord? And the Lord said, I am Jesus whom thou persecutest: it is hard for thee to kick against the pricks. And he trembling and astonished said, Lord, what wilt thou have me to do? And the Lord said unto him, Arise, and go into the city, and it shall be told thee what thou must do. And the men which journeyed with him stood speechless, hearing a voice, but seeing no man. And Saul arose from the earth; and when his eyes were opened, he saw no man: but they led him by the hand, and brought him into Damascus.

Acts 22:6-11
And it came to pass, that, as I made my journey, and was come

nigh unto Damascus about noon, suddenly there shone from heaven a great light round about me. And I fell unto the ground, and heard a voice saying unto me, Saul, Saul, why persecutest thou me? And I answered, Who art thou, Lord? And he said unto me, I am Jesus of Nazareth, whom thou persecutest. And they that were with me saw indeed the light, and were afraid; but they understood not the voice of him that spake to me. And I said, What shall I do, LORD? And the Lord said unto me, Arise, and go into Damascus; and there it shall be told thee of all things which are appointed for thee to do. And when I could not see for the glory of that light, being led by the hand of them that were with me, I came into Damascus.

Observations on these passages:

1. Paul and the men saw the light, though no one saw to whom the voice which was speaking belonged.

2. Paul saw the glory of the light, and it was so intense he was blinded by it, but the men with him did not even see it in the same intense way he did.

3. Paul heard and understood the voice that was speaking

4. The men heard the voice that was speaking, but did not understand it

In this case the vision was waking. What is most interesting is that the vision was experienced in one way by Paul, and in another, more limited way, by the men with him. This implies that it is possible for a group of people to experience the same vision. Yet, this case also shows that one person can see A but another person can see B, even while they are both having a shared Vision.
So it seems an angel could cause several people to have a Vision at the same time, but each person might see something different, still experiencing it with their bodily senses, but differently for each person.

Dreams Caused by Angels

Besides Visions, the Bible teaches that angels can also cause dreams, such as seeing an angel in a dream, as is in the case of Joseph the husband of Mary, surrogate father of Jesus Christ:

Matt 1:20 But while he thought on these things, behold, **the angel of the Lord appeared unto him in a dream**, saying, Joseph, thou son of David, fear not to take unto thee Mary thy wife: for that which is conceived in her is of the Holy Ghost.
Matt 2:13 And when they were departed, behold, **the angel of the Lord appeareth to Joseph in a dream**, saying, Arise, and take the young child and his mother, and flee into Egypt, and be thou there until I bring thee word: for Herod will seek the young child to destroy him.

The Bible also gives an example that some experiences may be a mix between a dream and a vision, but happen when one is asleep in one's bed. "In a **dream**, in a **vision** of the night, when deep sleep falleth upon men, in slumberings upon the bed" Job 33:15

The Abilities of Fallen Angels as Described in the Bible

Chapter 2 - Physical Manifestations, and Physical Interactions During Visions

Physical Interactions with Angels

Besides Dreams and Visions, the Bible teaches that angels can also interact with people physically, in ways that leave physical effects afterwards.

Acts 12:5-12, 18-19
Peter therefore was kept in prison: but prayer was made without ceasing of the church unto God for him. And when Herod would have brought him forth, the same night Peter was sleeping between two soldiers, bound with two chains: and the keepers before the door kept the prison. **And, behold, the angel of the Lord came upon him, and a light shined in the prison**: and he smote Peter on the side, and raised him up, saying, Arise up quickly. And his chains fell off from his hands. And the angel said unto him, Gird thyself, and bind on thy sandals. And so he did. And he saith unto him, Cast thy garment about thee, and follow me. And he went out, and followed him; **and wist not that it was true which was done by the angel; but thought he saw a vision**. When they were past the first and the second ward, they came unto the iron gate that leadeth unto the city; which opened to them of his own accord: and they went out, and passed on through one street; and forthwith the angel departed from him. And when Peter was come to himself, he said,
Now I know of a surety, that the LORD hath sent his angel, and hath delivered me out of the hand of Herod, and from all the expectation of the people of the Jews. And when he had considered the thing, he came to the house of Mary the mother of John, whose surname was Mark; where many were gathered together praying. …. Now as soon as it was day, there was no small stir among the soldiers, what was become of Peter. And when Herod had sought for him, and found him not, he examined

the keepers, and commanded that they should be put to death. And he went down from Judaea to Caesarea, and there abode.

In this case an angel is sent to free Peter from Herod's prison. At first Peter thinks he is experiencing a vision, but soon realizes these events have truly taken place. Peter had visions before, and his confusion proves the point that *visions are real to the bodily senses - as real as objective reality -* which is why Peter was not sure if what was happening was a vision or not.
But the events were physically real and did take place in objective reality.

The angel materialized in a physical way and caused lasting physical changes in objective reality. Other people, such as the guards, Herod, and Peter's friends, were all affected by these lasting physical changes to objective reality, in the angel rescuing Peter from prison.

Not only that, but the angel was able to defy physics in objective reality, or seem to have supernatural powers, by doing things such as causing a light to shine, chains to fall off, likely opening what was a locked gate, and moving a very heavy door with apparently supernatural strength, as well as appearing and disappearing seemingly out of nowhere.

Another example of angels appearing physically and leaving physical effects is Gen 19:

Gen 19:1-7, 10-13, 24-28
And there came two angels to Sodom at even; and Lot sat in the gate of Sodom: and Lot seeing them rose up to meet them; and he bowed himself with his face toward the ground; And he said, Behold now, my lords, turn in, I pray you, into your servant's house, and tarry all night, and wash your feet, and ye shall rise up early, and go on your ways.
And they said, Nay; but we will abide in the street all night. And he pressed upon them greatly; and they turned in unto him, and entered into his house; and he made them a feast, and did bake unleavened bread, and they did eat. But before they lay down, the men of the city, even the men of Sodom, compassed the house

round, both old and young, all the people from every quarter: And they called unto Lot, and said unto him, Where are the men which came in to thee this night? bring them out unto us, that we may know them. And Lot went out at the door unto them, and shut the door after him, And said, I pray you, brethren, do not so wickedly....But the men put forth their hand, and pulled Lot into the house to them, and shut to the door. And they smote the men that were at the door of the house with blindness, both small and great: so that they wearied themselves to find the door. And the men said unto Lot, Hast thou here any besides? son in law, and thy sons, and thy daughters, and whatsoever thou hast in the city, bring them out of this place: **For we will destroy this place**, because the cry of them is waxen great before the face of the LORD; **and the LORD hath sent us to destroy it**...Then the LORD rained upon Sodom and upon Gomorrah brimstone and fire from the LORD out of heaven; And he overthrew those cities, and all the plain, and all the inhabitants of the cities, and that which grew upon the ground. But his wife looked back from behind him, and she became a pillar of salt. And Abraham gat up early in the morning to the place where he stood before the LORD: And he looked toward Sodom and Gomorrah, and toward all the land of the plain, and beheld, and, lo, the smoke of the country went up as the smoke of a furnace.

Some observations: All of the men of the city could see the angels, not just Lot. The angels caused all the men who were harassing Lot to become blind. The angels likely turned Lot's wife into a pillar of salt. The angels also destroyed the city of Sodom and Gomorrah, and Abraham was able to observe the smoke from the city's destruction from far away. Today some people (see arkdiscovery.com) say they have found the destroyed city, and no doubt some evidence of this angelic event remains to this day, somewhere.

In the case of Sodom and Gomorrah the angels were seen by men and interacted with them. These angels appeared looking as human men. However, angels can also interact with objective reality without being seen, and remaining invisible, as is seen in Job.

Job 1:12-19 And the LORD said unto Satan, Behold, all that he hath is in thy power; only upon himself put not forth thine hand. So Satan went forth from the presence of the LORD.
And there was a day when his sons and his daughters were eating and drinking wine in their eldest brother's house: And there came a messenger unto Job, and said, The oxen were plowing, and the asses feeding beside them: And the Sabeans fell upon them, and took them away; yea, they have slain the servants with the edge of the sword; and I only am escaped alone to tell thee. While he was yet speaking, there came also another, and said, The fire of God is fallen from heaven, and hath burned up the sheep, and the servants, and consumed them; and I only am escaped alone to tell thee. While he was yet speaking, there came also another, and said, The Chaldeans made out three bands, and fell upon the camels, and have carried them away, yea, and slain the servants with the edge of the sword; and I only am escaped alone to tell thee. While he was yet speaking, there came also another, and said, Thy sons and thy daughters were eating and drinking wine in their eldest brother's house: And, behold, there came a great wind from the wilderness, and smote the four corners of the house, and it fell upon the young men, and they are dead; and I only am escaped alone to tell thee.

In this case God effectively removed a "hedge of protection" around Job and allowed everything but Job's life to be put "into Satan's hands" (Job 1:12). Satan then inspired people to kill Job's servants, caused a fire from heaven to come down and kill his sheep and servants, and caused a great wind to demolish a house on top of Job's children, killing them all. Though Satan was invisible in all of these events, nevertheless the events Satan caused occurred in objective reality, and there were multiple witnesses to the physical effects of what had occurred.

Another lasting effect angels can cause is physical illness or injury, is seen in Acts and in Job:

Acts 12:21-23 And upon a set day Herod, arrayed in royal apparel, sat upon his throne, and made an oration unto them. And the people gave a shout, saying, It is the voice of a god, and not of a man. And immediately the angel of the Lord smote him, because he gave not God the glory: and he was eaten of worms, and died.

In this case in Acts the angel was invisible, at least his public appearance to the crowd is not recorded, and the angel caused a physical ailment resulting in death to the body of a person.

Job 2:6-7 And the LORD said unto Satan, Behold, he is in thine hand; but save his life. So went Satan forth from the presence of the LORD, and smote Job with sore boils from the sole of his foot unto his crown.

In Job, the angel Satan was invisible, but in objective reality he caused real and visible injury/disease to Job's body, and Job was ill for some time, until God set things right.

In the case of fallen angels, such as the fallen cherubim Satan, we also know that they can appear looking like holy angels (who look like men).

And no marvel; for Satan himself is transformed into an angel of light. 2 Cor 11:13

Holy angels are of the messenger-type of angel, who look like men, though sometimes glowing with light. Satan who is a cherubim (with 4 faces, 3 of animals, and 4 wings) can transform himself to appear as looking like a Holy messenger-type angel, like a man and glowing with light. And of course fallen messenger-type angels, who already look like men, can do this all the more easily.

Observations on Physical Interactions with angels:
1. There can be multiple witnesses of angels who appear looking like men
2. There can be multiple witnesses to lasting physical effects caused by angels, including illnesses, injury, and death
3. There can be supernatural occurrences that seem to defy physics, in objective reality
4. Generally reality follows normal physical laws, except for the actions of the angels
5. Physical effects can also be caused by angels that, though

present, remain invisible
6. Fallen angels can appear looking like holy angels, who look like men, sometimes glowing

So far we have covered that the Bible teaches that angels can interact with people by the methods of Visions, Dreams, and can interact with people physically either while appearing as men, or while remaining invisible. The Bible also teaches that there can be limited physical interactions during a Vision that seem to combine or merge with the Vision experience itself. These limited physical interactions can leave physical effects that remain after the Vision is over.

Visions Caused by Angels Can Include Limited Physical Interactions Which Can Leave Physical Aftereffects

Let's look at an example from the book of Revelation. The entire book of Revelation contains a very long and detailed Vision given to John by a Holy angel, even though some of the terminology seems a little different at first glance,
Rev 17:3 So **he carried me away in the spirit** into the wilderness: and I saw a woman sit upon a scarlet coloured beast, full of names of blasphemy, having seven heads and ten horns.
Rev 21:10 And **he carried me away in the spirit** to a great and high mountain, and shewed me that great city, the holy Jerusalem, descending out of heaven from God,

In these examples John says that "he carried me away in the spirit". The "he" that is referenced here is an angel of the Lord, a messenger of Jesus Christ, and this is established in Rev 22:8-9
And I John saw these things, and heard [them]. And when I had heard and seen, I fell down to worship before the feet of <u>the angel which shewed me these things</u>. Then saith he unto me, See [thou do it] not: for I am thy fellow servant, and of thy brethren the prophets, and of them which keep the sayings of this book: worship God.

From these passages, we know that all the things John experienced in the Vision were caused by a Holy angel. An angel can "carry someone away in the spirit", but this term is synonymous with someone having a Vision caused by an angel. We can know the term is synonymous because John also makes clear that all of this was a Vision:
And thus I saw the horses **in the vision**, and them that sat on them, having breastplates of fire, and of jacinth, and brimstone: and the heads of the horses [were] as the heads of lions; and out of their mouths issued fire and smoke and brimstone. Rev 9:17

Altogether, the entire imagery John recorded in the book of Revelation was caused by an angel of the Lord showing John these things in a Vision. Also, the same phrases are used in Eze 11:24, "Afterwards the spirit took me up, and brought me in a vision by the Spirit of God into Chaldea, to them of the captivity. So the vision that I had seen went up from me."
And so if one is "in the spirit", then the Bible indicates that one is having a Vision.

What John experienced was real to all the bodily senses, even including taste, and internal feeling in his stomach, as John perceived he was experiencing all this bodily. John ate a scroll which was part of the vision, tasted it, and it was "bitter to his stomach".
And I took the little book out of the angel's hand, and ate it up; and it was in my mouth sweet as honey: and as soon as I had eaten it, my belly was bitter. Rev 10:10

In this Vision caused by a Holy angel, John was writing down what he saw and heard throughout his entire experience on a piece of paper.
Saying, I am Alpha and Omega, the first and the last: and, What thou seest, write in a book, and send [it] unto the seven churches which are in Asia; unto Ephesus, and unto Smyrna, and unto Pergamos, and unto Thyatira, and unto Sardis, and unto Philadelphia, and unto Laodicea…Write the things which thou hast seen, and the things which are, and the things which shall be hereafter; Rev 1:11,19

And when the seven thunders had uttered their voices, I was about to write: and I heard a voice from heaven saying unto me, Seal up those things which the seven thunders uttered, and write them not. Rev 10:4

John did not write down the Vision experience after it had ended, but while it was ongoing. What is astounding is that this paper remained with him after the experience had ended. Whether John was given the paper to write on and the writing instrument during the Vision, or if John carried these things into the experience and out of the experience later, is unknown. But in either case, John took the paper out of the Vision with him, which he had written on during the Vision, and so a greater level of lasting physical effects is shown here than in most Visions.

This example establishes that the Bible teaches an angel can cause a person to have a Vision which leaves minor physical effects or traces, like the scroll John recorded the Vision on, or even bodily effects, even internal bodily effects like his stomach becoming bitter. The Bible also teaches that angels can have physical interactions with people that can include causing people bodily injuries or illness. As Visions can include limited physical interactions with angels that leave physical aftereffects, it makes sense that Visions could possibly include physical aftereffects of injuries or illness as well.

The Abilities of Fallen Angels as Described in the Bible

Chapter 3 – Visions: Time Perception Manipulation, Extreme Realness, and Wide Variety of Possible Content

<u>Visions Caused by Angels
Can Manipulate a Person's Perception of Time</u>

A Vision also may include elements of a fallen angel manipulating a person's perception of time. Another angelic encounter in a passage with similar terminology to "carried me away" uses the phrase "took him up". These may be synonymous terms. This experience caused by an angel (Satan) was likely also a Vision experience.

And **the devil took him up**, to a high mountain, and showed him all the kingdoms of the world <u>in a moment of time</u> Luke 4:5 (Compare And he carried me away in the spirit, to a great and high mountain, and shewed me that great city, the holy Jerusalem, descending out of heaven from God Rev 21:10)

The Greek word here for 'moment' is "stigme" (4743) which literally means a "point" of time. This word is used only once in the New Testament, but is used in the Greek Old Testament, the Septuagint, in Isaiah 29:5. The word that is translated as "stigme" is "petha`" (6621) in Hebrew. According to Thayer's Lexicon, "petha" means "the opening of the eyes", hence the meaning "a moment of time". The amount of time referenced to here is the amount of time it takes to open your eyes. This is no more than the time it would take to blink. It takes a human about 300 to 400 milliseconds to blink; that is 3/10ths to 4/10ths of 1 second.

How could Jesus see "all the kingdoms of the world" in the time it takes to blink? Or even in one full second? It would seem that to be shown all the kingdoms of the world should take at least a couple hours, if not days, if a thorough tour was done. But even snapshot pictures in quick succession would take a couple minutes, and this without any time to really think about what one was seeing. And so the necessary amount of time to be shown all the kingdoms of the world is still incredibly more than 3/10ths of a second, or even one full second.

This passage implies that one second passed in time, but Jesus experienced subjectively a much longer period of time than one second during that one second. And so it's possible that there can be time perception manipulation in a Vision caused (in particular) by a fallen angel. There is another example in the Bible of something similar on a greater scale, during Joshua's Long Day.

Then spake Joshua to the LORD in the day when the LORD delivered up the Amorites before the children of Israel, and he said in the sight of Israel, Sun, stand thou still upon Gibeon; and thou, Moon, in the valley of Ajalon. And the sun stood still, and the moon stayed, until the people had avenged themselves upon their enemies. Is not this written in the book of Jasher? So the sun stood still in the midst of heaven, and hasted not to go down about a whole day. And there was no day like that before it or after it, that the LORD hearkened unto the voice of a man: for the LORD fought for Israel. Josh 10:12-14

This passage could be interpreted as to mean that God can pause the progress of time forward, that the clock is paused, but people still can do things while forward-moving time is paused. God seemed to be able to do this to the whole world, a large scale, as the sun stood still in the sky. Because the sun stood still in the sky, if time was being manipulated here (not the earth's rotation), then this was a case of forward-moving time being paused, and not a case of time travel. Yet while forward-moving time was paused, in that moment time in substance still seemed present, and in a way that still allowed people to interact and do things.

The angels are called "sons of God" or "gods" at times, and in this it seems they may be able to cause someone to perceive something similar on a very limited scale. The effect is that of a longer period of time being experienced during a much shorter period of time. But the only Biblical example of an angel doing this seems to be the fallen angel Satan doing this to Jesus alone, during what was very likely a Vision that Satan was causing Jesus to have. As a Vision, this was a spiritual experience that only affected the person having the Vision, and not everyone else in physical reality. The only Biblical example of a fallen angel being able to add time like this, is during a Vision the fallen angel is causing someone to have. But there is no indication or Biblical example that angels can do this on a larger scale like God Himself can do.

This makes sense as God made time (Gen 1:1), and is outside of it eternally. Only He is "the alpha and the omega the beginning and the end" (Rev 21:6, 22:13) and only God knows the end from the beginning (showing that angels cannot time travel):
Remember the former things of old: for I [am] God, and [there is] none else; [I am] God, and [there is] none like me, Declaring the end from the beginning, and from ancient times [the things] that are not [yet] done, saying, My counsel shall stand, and I will do all my pleasure: Isa 46:9-10

Angels and Fallen angels are still only created beings who experience linear time as we do, caught in the flow of time moving forward.

But the prince of the kingdom of Persia withstood me one and twenty days: but, lo, Michael, one of the chief princes, came to help me; and I remained there with the kings of Persia. Dan 10:13

Therefore rejoice, [ye] heavens, and ye that dwell in them. Woe to the inhabiters of the earth and of the sea! for the devil is come down unto you, having great wrath, because he knoweth that he hath but a short time. Rev 12:12

And so while a fallen angel may be able to cause a person to perceive extra time in a Vision, while linear time seems to be paused, there is no indication that fallen angels can do this on a larger scale like God can. He is God who made time, and angels are just created beings who exist caught in the flow of time. And as this could be confusing, I hope that it has been made clear that this does not have anything to do with the science fiction concept of time travel, which in fact the Bible indicates that fallen angels cannot do, and is not possible.

However, the Bible does seem to indicate that a longer time can be condensed into a shorter time, like time itself has a second aspect or dimension to it.

But, beloved, be not ignorant of this one thing, that one day [is] with the Lord as a thousand years, and a thousand years as one day. The Lord is not slack concerning his promise, as some men count slackness; but is longsuffering to us-ward, not willing that any should perish, but that all should come to repentance. 2 Pet 3:8-9

A thousand of our years can seem a short time to God, who is eternal. A thousand years for us doesn't seem like a long time to Him, but rather a thousand of our years seems to Him like a day would for us. But also, just one of our days, as perceived by Him, would seem to us to stretch on and on like it was taking a thousand years, from our perspective. This may be as in a single one of our days, the Lord is so busy and with so much to do, that it would take us a thousand years to get as much done. It might take us a thousand years to get as much done as He does in a day. This may refer to what it is like, that He hears all of our prayers, and intercedes for all of us,
"Who [is] he that condemneth? [It is] Christ that died, yea rather, that is risen again, who is even at the right hand of God, <u>who also maketh intercession for us.</u>" Rom 8:34

All over the world, Jesus Christ intercedes for, and hears the prayers of millions of people, a multi-tasking of an incomprehensible sort. A solution in understanding this may be that a longer period of time can be condensed down into a shorter period. Time itself is a thing that was created by God, and may have been designed in such a way as to allow for this. But again, this is another Biblical example that a longer period of time can seem to be condensed into a shorter period of time. Time perception manipulation caused by the fallen angel Satan followed along these lines in the Vision he seemed to cause Jesus to have in Luke 4:5. And so the only sort of time manipulation that there is any Biblical precedent for is: time perception manipulation of adding time into a paused moment. Fallen angels seem to be able to do this in a limited way, and by the only example of this in the Bible, it seems they only can do this in a Vision they cause a person to experience.

A Vision Caused by an Angel Can Seem So Real As to be Indistinguishable from Reality

Peter couldn't tell if something was real or a Vision, and so in Acts mistook reality for a Vision, because Visions can seem so indistinguishably real.
Peter followed him (an angel) out of the prison, but he had no idea that what the angel was doing was really happening; he thought he was seeing a vision" Acts 10:9

There is a second witness to this by Paul. I believe in this example the Bible speaks on the difficulty of the confusion in telling one from the other, with guidance on how we should handle that difficulty.
It is not expedient for me doubtless to glory. I will come to **visions** and revelations of the Lord. I knew a man in Christ above fourteen years ago, (whether in the body, I cannot tell; or whether out of the body, I cannot tell: God knoweth;) such an one caught up to the third heaven. And I knew such a man, (whether in the body, or out of the body, I cannot tell: God knoweth;) How that he was caught up into paradise, and heard unspeakable words, which it is not lawful for a man to utter. 2 Corinthians 12:1-4

The word here for "caught up" is "harpazo", and the same word is used in Acts 8:39 when "the Spirit of the Lord caught away Philip, that the eunuch saw him no more". And so being "caught up" does happen to be a term that can refer to the Holy Spirit moving someone to a new place, bodily. It is used in reference to Jesus' ascension (Rev 12:5) and to believers being caught up into the air to be with the Lord (1 Thes 4:17). And so this word seems to reference more to people being transported by God bodily.

But on the other hand, Paul also makes it very clear that he cannot tell if the man was caught up 'in his body' to the third heaven, or caught up 'out of his body' to the third heaven. To understand what Paul means here by "out of the body", we have to look to earlier in this same book, in 2 Cor 5:4-9, where Paul says, "We are confident, [I say], and willing rather to be absent from the body, and to be present with the Lord." In this case Paul references to one whose body is dead, and so their spirit is with the Lord. Paul defines the term "out of the body" to mean one is "in spirit".

And so in 2 Cor 12 Paul references back to 2 Cor 5, saying he did not know if the man was "out of his body" which is another way to say "in spirit". Putting this together what Paul says is that he doesn't know if the man was caught up to the third heaven in his body, or in his spirit.

The word "harpazo" and term "caught up" is rather synonymous with "carried away" or "taken up", and these are terms which are both used of Visions caused by angels. And indeed, in this passage Paul is referencing to "**visions** and revelations of the Lord".

In 2 Cor 5 Paul is saying that he doesn't know if this man was caught up bodily to the third heaven, or if the man was caught up in the spirit to the third heaven in a Vision caused by a Holy angel. Many people think Paul was referring to himself in this passage, though this also may have been a story he heard in detail from whoever experience it. In any case, Paul couldn't figure out if the experience happened bodily, or was a Vision in the spirit. The reason why Paul couldn't figure out which was the case is because a Vision experience seems so real that it can be indistinguishable from reality.

2 Cor 12 is telling us that it can be impossible to tell by the bodily senses if something was a physical bodily experience, or if it just seemed to be and was a Vision in the spirit. However, as much as Paul admits he does not know if this man was caught up to the third heaven in his body or in his spirit, Paul also makes it very clear that God knows. This means only God has the answers, for instance in His Word, and through His Holy Spirit. We cannot tell with our bodily senses alone whether an experience was in the body, or a Vision, but God can tell. While people sometimes can't

figure out whether an experience was real or a Vision, God can reveal the truth about an experience to those who ask Him.

If a person is "carried away in the spirit" while having a vision caused by an angel, does this mean that a person's spirit leaves their body?

No. The Bible indicates that a person who is having a Vision, taken in the spirit, actually never leaves their body. Daniel had "visions of his head upon his bed" and in the middle of the vision "was grieved in my spirit in the midst of [my] body, and the visions of my head troubled me." (Dan 7:1,15) And so we can see that while Daniel had Visions, in his spirit, that this was all in the midst of his own body (no matter where he seemed to be, or what he saw) and that the Visions he experienced were of his head, which is part of his body. Not only that, but all of these Visions Daniel had took place while <u>he never left his bed</u>. Note that part of this vision included Daniel seeing the "Ancient of Days", likely on His throne, which would be in the third heaven.

Even though a person may seem to be somewhere else, they actually are only "carried in the spirit" in the "midst of their body". The Visions are of their head, in their spirit, which is in their body. So the Bible indicates their spirit never leaves their body, but they have the Vision experience in their spirit, and their spirit remains inside of their body.

<u>Visions Caused by Angels Can Contain Just About Anything</u>

Visions can include settings or landscapes of just about any place, be about anything, and can include anyone or anything as a character in the Vision, and can include perception of travel.

Daniel had a Vision that occurred where he stood by the River Chaldea. Peter had a Vision while on the housetop where he was, of the housetop, though he was in a trance. So Visions can be of places that are a person's normal surroundings. John had a Vision where he saw heaven, as did Isaiah (Isa 6) and Daniel (Dan 7), and so a Vision could be of Heaven.

Ezekiel saw a Vision of Jerusalem, of the temple, which was a real place. Ezekiel also had a Vision of a valley full of bones, and when the bones came to life into an army, this was not of something taking place in an actual valley somewhere (Eze 37). And so Visions can be of real places or invented places. Even if the valley was a real valley somewhere, what Ezekiel saw was not actually taking place in that valley. Though, what Ezekiel saw in Jerusalem was taking place there. So Visions can be of things that are happening somewhere, or of things that are not actually happening somewhere (but are symbolic, and of truth being taught only in the case of visions from Holy angels).

Ezekiel experienced the perception of travel in a Vision (Eze 8, Eze 40), and Daniel seemed to be near a great sea in his Vision (Dan 7) and so Visions can seem to include travel or being in a different location. But Daniel makes clear he didn't go anywhere during his Visions, but was in his bed while he had them.

Ezekiel saw people in the Vision of the valley of bones. John saw people in his Vision of Revelation, as well as strange looking locust creatures, angels, a dragon, a strange beast with seven heads and the body parts of various animals. The characters in a Vision could be in the forms of people, real or not, angels, animals that exist, and strange creatures that don't exist. But like an artist can draw a cartoon of about anything, or any place, so can an angel cause a Vision to contain just about any landscape or characters.

What is seen in a Vision can vary wildly and be of just about anything. During a Vision a person may see angels, people, entities, living creatures, landscapes of strange places, or of familiar ones, as well as perceiving they experience travel to various places. Yet all of this is just part of the Vision caused by the angel, and the Bible teaches, like Daniel, that people don't actually go anywhere, regardless of what they perceive during a Vision.

The Abilities of Fallen Angels as Described in the Bible

Chapter 4 - Summary of Visions, and False Visions Caused by Fallen Angels

<u>The Bible summarily teaches several things about Visions caused by angels:</u>

1. A Vision can seem totally real to a single bodily sense (like sight) or to all of the bodily senses, and a person's self-perception is usually that they are in their body.

2. A Vision can affect one person or multiple people, though they may perceive it differently

3. A Vision can occur in a waking state, or in a trance state

4. A Vision can be causes by a visible angel, or an invisible angel

5. A Vision can involve some physical effects that remain afterwards, such as objects that remain with a person, and bodily effects, even internal ones.

6. A Vision can involve manipulation of a person's perception of time, like an hour in a minute.

7. A Vision can contain just about any landscape, or any sort of characters, and can seem to involve travel, even though the person doesn't actually go anywhere

8. A Vision can seem so real to the bodily senses that it is indistinguishable from reality, even in the case of people who are experienced with Visions, though God knows and can reveal the truth

This level of power in the hands of fallen angels is staggering to conceptualize. I thank God that they are limited in what they can do, and who they can do it to, by God's laws of spiritual authority grounds. A fallen angel can only attack someone if they have spiritual authority grounds and rights to do so. God places a "hedge of protection" around people, limiting whom the fallen angels can harass and harm, and limiting the level of harassment and the extent of the harm that they can do to a person. (See Job 1 and 2, also the New Testament is full of this concept. This also involves the concept of spiritual warfare, see Resources at end for further information.) It is also a relief to know that for every fallen angel, there are 2 Holy angels working for God and Jesus; and so the fallen angels are outnumbered two to one. Additionally Jesus Christ assures believers in Him:

Behold, I give unto you power to tread on serpents and scorpions, and over all the power of the enemy: and nothing shall by any means hurt you. Luke 10:19

False Dreams and False Visions caused by Fallen Angels

We have covered Visions that were had by people who were prophets, or those with the gift of the Holy Spirit of prophecy, such as Daniel, John, Ezekiel, Peter and Paul. Even in the case of Joseph having a dream of an angel, telling him to flee to Egypt, this also was a prophetic warning given by a Holy angel. When Holy angels cause people to have a dream or a Vision they are delivering a message, but often these messages are classified by the Bible as "prophecy" and those who have them as "prophets".

In the Bible, prophecy is heavily associated with a person having dreams or Visions. And as we have established, dreams and Visions can be caused by Holy angels, who are God's messengers.

"And it shall come to pass in the last days, saith God, I will pour out of my Spirit upon all flesh: and your sons and your daughters shall prophesy, and your young men shall see visions, and your old men shall dream dreams" Acts 2:17

"And he said, Hear now my words: If there be a <u>prophet</u> among you, [I] the LORD will make myself known unto him in a <u>vision</u>, [and] will speak unto him in a <u>dream</u>." Num 12:6

And so a person who has a dream or a Vision caused by a Holy angel is classified by the Bible as a prophet. And while an angel delivers a message to the prophet, the prophet in turn delivers the message on to other people. The Strong's definition of prophet is a "spokesman, speaker", and to prophesy is to " a) be under the influence of a divine spirit" or to be "b) a false prophet".

The Bible also mentions false prophets. True prophets have true Visions that are caused by Holy angels sent by God. But the Bible teaches that false prophets have False Visions and Vain Visions.

"Have ye not seen a <u>vain vision</u>, and have ye not spoken a <u>lying divination</u>, whereas ye say, The LORD saith [it]; albeit I have not spoken? Therefore thus saith the Lord GOD; Because ye have spoken vanity, and seen lies, therefore, behold, I [am] against you, saith the Lord GOD. And mine hand shall be upon <u>the prophets that see vanity</u>, and that divine lies: they shall not be in the assembly of my people, neither shall they be written in the writing of the house of Israel, neither shall they enter into the land of Israel; and ye shall know that I [am] the Lord GOD." Eze 13:7-9

Then the LORD said unto me, <u>The prophets prophesy lies</u> in my name: I sent them not, neither have I commanded them, neither spake unto them: they prophesy unto you a <u>false vision and divination</u>, and a thing of nought, and the deceit of their heart. Jer 14:14

False prophets have False Visions, and these are caused by Fallen angels who lie and deceive.

And he saith, `Therefore, hear a word of the Lord; I have seen the Lord sitting on His throne, and all <u>the host of the heavens [angels]</u> standing by Him, on His right and on His left; and the Lord saith, Who doth entice Ahab, and he doth go up and fall in Ramoth-Gilead? and this one saith thus, and that one is saying thus. `And a spirit came out, and stood before the Lord, and saith, I -- I do entice him; and the Lord saith unto him, By what? and he saith, I go out, and have been <u>a spirit of falsehood in the mouth of</u>

<u>all his prophets</u>; and He saith, Thou dost entice, and also thou art able; go out and do so. 1 Kin 22:19-22

In this passage the angels were around God's throne, and an angel admits to having been communicating deception or lies to the false prophets. God permissively allows this deceptive angel to continue to do what the falling angel himself is able to do, and chooses to do. And so the Bible teaches that fallen angels do communicate lies and deception to false prophets. And this is by the method of false dreams and False Visions, which false prophets are reported to have.

Beyond false messages which fallen angels can communicate in False Visions or dreams, they can also use False Visions and dreams to simply harass and frighten people, to a terrible extent. While Job was under a series of attacks caused by Satan, a fallen angel, Job records:

When I say, My bed shall comfort me, my couch shall ease my complaint; Then you <u>scare me with dreams</u> and <u>terrify me with visions </u>so that I would choose strangling and death rather than my bones. Job 7:13-15

And so the Bible teaches that fallen angels can victimize people with their ability to cause dreams and Visions, using these to scare and terrify, even to the point of severe traumatization from them. Job here experiences severe depression, longing to die rather than deal with these terrifying dreams and Visions. It seems various other psychological symptoms besides severe depression could result from these experiences as well, as Job's account here shows they can be very traumatic, and different people handle trauma in different ways.

Along with this, fallen angels can also cause False Dreams and False Visions to communicate a lying or deceptive message, false information, to a person with the intent that the person might become a false prophet, who shares the false message as truth.

This is part of why the Bible warns that people must test spirits, not just believe them, as these fallen angels are at war against all of humanity, to deceive us:

"Beloved, believe not every spirit, but try the spirits whether they are of God: because many false prophets are gone out into the world." (1 Jn 4:1) and as Jesus said, "Many false prophets will arise, and will mislead many." (Matt 24:11)

But even in the midst of this war followers of Jesus Christ can have God's reassurance,
Yet in all these things we are more than conquerors through Him who loved us. For I am persuaded that neither death nor life, nor angels, nor principalities nor powers [fallen angels], nor things present nor things to come, nor height nor depth, nor any other created thing, shall be able to separate us from the love of God which is in Christ Jesus our Lord. Rom 8:37-39

Chapter 5 - Alien Abduction Experiences
False Visions and Terrifying Dreams

Next we will compare modern alien abduction accounts to the Biblically based abilities of Fallen angels. The Bible teaches that Fallen angels can cause False dreams and False Visions.

In False Visions causes by Fallen angels:

1. A Vision can seem totally real to a single bodily sense (like sight) or to all of the bodily senses, and a person's self-perception is usually that they are in their body.
2. A Vision can affect one person or multiple people, though they may perceive it differently
3. A Vision can occur in a waking state, or in a trance state
4. A Vision can be causes by a visible angel, or an invisible angel
5. A Vision can involve some physical effects that remain afterwards, such as objects that remain with a person, and bodily effects, even internal ones.
6. A Vision can involve manipulation of a person's perception of time, like an hour in a minute.
7. A Vision can contain just about any landscape, or any sort of characters, and can seem to involve travel, even though the person doesn't actually go anywhere
8. A Vision can seem so real to the bodily senses that it is indistinguishable from reality, even in the case of people who are experienced with Visions, though God knows and can reveal the truth

What is experienced in "alien abduction" accounts?

Abductees report in their experiences that in some cases the experience feels completely real to the bodily senses, sight, hearing, touch, taste, smell, and time perception. Abductees can be adamant that some of these experiences were NOT dreams, but occurred in a waking state. Here are some common events in abductee accounts:

Seeing aliens of a wide variety of types

Walking through walls (themselves or seeing aliens do so)

Defying gravity (flying or floating themselves, or seeing aliens/spacecraft do so)

Travel to outer-space, other planets, and other galaxies, with no suit or spacecraft, and Travel to outerspace in spacecraft

Impossible scenarios, like breathing underwater or in viscous liquid, without drowning

Not breathing for a half hour or more in air, without suffocating or dying

Electromagnetic disturbances, electronic malfunctions

Alice in wonderland sorts of landscapes

Aliens' bodies shape-shifting into new forms

Injuries that only last until the end of the experience

Injuries that remain after the experience, sometimes mostly healed and leaving scars

Strange or rare illnesses

Medical-like examinations and procedures including needles and drills

Time perception disturbances and manipulation, time loss, time gain

Sexual molestation, assault and rape

Miscarriages and false pregnancies with supernatural aspects

Physical pain and torture

Partial or complete paralysis during experience

As you can see, these experiences are often highly confusing, painful, and violating.

Now let's look at some individual alien abductee accounts.

The case of "Robert" summarized from CE4 Research Group's case files:
On a Monday, Joe and Robert had a conversation. Robert said he had been having abduction experiences with colorful light beings for a year. Each being was a different color, and looked much like the light-people in the movie Cocoon. He described that it felt real to his bodily senses, and he seemed in his body, however he did not need to breathe during his experiences.
Later that week, on Thursday, Robert was in a car with his girlfriend. Robert slumped over like he passed out unconscious while in the car, and his girlfriend was with him. Robert experienced a long period of conscious time during what he later recounted as being like a vision with the beings. He felt he seemed to have gone somewhere else. However, to Robert's girlfriend, he was in a trance state that only lasted a minute or so. But he experienced several hours' worth of experiences, during the minute he was passed out. As his girlfriend was there with him, she saw he did not go anywhere, his body did not leave. Just in that week, since first talking to Joe, the experiences had turned very bad, and the light-beings were being very nasty to him, and Robert wanted the experiences to stop. Robert could somehow feel that an experience was about to happen, before it happened, precipitating the entities attacks on him. Telling his girlfriend beforehand, Robert had a second experience the same evening.
-Joe Jordan, CE4Research, Unholy Communion: The Unwanted Piece of the UFO Puzzle www.ce4research.com

Robert said he had been having abduction experiences with colorful light beings much like the light-people in the movie Cocoon. He described that it felt real to his bodily senses, and that he seemed to be in his body; however he did not need to breathe during his experiences.

Robert had 2 experiences while seeming to pass out in a trance, which seemed to last hours for him, but his girlfriend said he was only in this state for a few minutes.

(Robert Continued)
Afterwards, Robert called Joe, telling him what had been happening to him that day. While on the phone, Robert could feel another attack coming on. This was the third experience that day, and he was again in a trance state, for a couple of minutes. His girlfriend, present, saw this, and talked to Joe on the phone while this was ongoing. When Robert's experience ended, he got back on the phone and related to Joe that the beings who were attacking Robert told Robert that they "hated Joe" because he understood what was happening to Robert.

The next morning Joe and a Christian co-worker went to Robert's house and met with him and his girlfriend. While there, Robert felt another attack coming on, but before he was forced into a trance again, they rebuked the entities in the name and authority of Jesus Christ, and Robert said he could feel the entities disappear, stopping the attack.
-Joe Jordan, CE4Research, Unholy Communion: The Unwanted Piece of the UFO Puzzle www.ce4research.com

As I mentioned earlier, time manipulation seems to occur in the Bible during False Visions caused by fallen angels. In this case, the experience could have been a False Vision, and matches the Biblical description very well. Robert experienced time manipulation, and the experiences were real to his bodily senses, and at the same time during his experiences he did not breathe for impossibly long periods of time (that is, his subjective time).

The case of Robert was of a False Vision which was real to the bodily senses, it fully overlaid objective reality, happened in a waking trance state, to one person. But there was a witness with Robert that saw him go into a trance state, and remained with him throughout. This shows, as is recorded in Daniel, that he did not go anywhere, but rather had these False Visions in his spirit, in his body, while remaining where he was.

This next case from an "alien abductee" is from "Taken: Inside the Alien-Human Abduction Agenda" by the late Dr. Karla Turner PhD.

"Lisa had some conscious memories of encounters with the typical Grays, as well as missing-time episodes, multiple-witnessed UFO sightings, unexplained body marks, telepathic communications from unseen sources, and many dream-memories of ambiguous reality - except in those instances where other evidence pointed to an actual event. While the details of Lisa's life-long involvement are certainly very typical, the alien intrusions are clearly more intense and frequent than in many such cases...

In 1980, however, Lisa did see something very different from the shadows, in a terrifying event. "A being appeared to me," she recalled, "when I was a couple of weeks pregnant. We had just got into bed and Neal already seemed 'out of it,' and the being appeared on the end of the bed, squatting, telling me mentally the child I was carrying was special and it would be a boy. I almost had a fainting spell. I threw the covers over my head as the being was leaping toward me, I believe, and said, 'In Jesus' name, take it away!' It disappeared, and I fell quickly asleep. It was about three feet tall, dark-skinned, leathery looking. I don't remember anything else."
-Karla Turner PhD, Taken: Inside the Alien-Human Abduction Agenda, Pg. 36-37

I would also say this case was a False Vision, partially overlaying objective reality, in a waking state, and happening to one person. When rebuked in Jesus' name the False Vision ended, and what she was seeing disappeared.

Transcribed from the Cursed Net internet radio show, the next case describes multiple witnesses seeing a UFO over a populated area.

"<u>Byron</u>: That beings me to the question of when did you first see a UFO? And how did it affect you?
<u>Kathy</u>: The first UFO I saw I was probably in my very early 20s, there were three other people with me and we all saw it, only one

of them remembers seeing it, and none of us remember what we did the rest of the day…

Byron: How could you forget such a strange instance, and its also puzzling to me how you could not remember what you did for the rest of the day, after an event like that, could that indicate this expression called "missing time", may have taken place right at that time?

Kathy: That's what I'm taking for granted now… I mean we had a long drive home, a couple of hours from where we were at the time, and none of us remember, we don't even remember that weekend, I mean the next few days we all went, "What did we do Saturday? I don't remember." You know, but it gets fuzzier and fuzzier as the years go on…

Byron: What did it look like?

Kathy: It was huge, we were on a street with houses on both sides that backed up to a beach, and we were walking to our vehicles, and it came over us, and the reason I think we looked up is because it got dark, it was like the sun went away, and you could see the bottom of a … the starship enterprise, it was like mechanical looking stuff on the bottom, but you couldn't see the beginning or the end of it, you could see it went past the houses on that side of the street, it went past the houses on [the other] that side of the street, as far as you could see in both directions, up and down, its like we were seeing just a teeny piece of the bottom of a huge spaceship… And there was virtually no sound either, that's something one of the other people who was with me said about it, because I remember us saying that "It's not making any sound at all" while we were looking up."

-Byron LeBeau, Richard Stout and Greg Messina,
 www.thecursednet.com, www.blogtalkradio.com/cursednet
with guest Kathy Land (1/5/09)

Happening in a populated area, in which a huge sun-blocking UFO would be arguably noticed by the residents, local police, and local news, this event seems more likely to be a False Vision than any sort of Physical Manifestation. This was a False Vision shared by a group of people, who were all under a deceptive attack with False Visions at the same time. This waking False Vision seemed to only partially overlay objective reality, in that the UFO was seen but not heard to make any sound at all, while hovering over the neighborhood. But there were multiple victims which saw the vision, and missing time was noted by all involved. Missing time is can be described as a type of time perception manipulation. All of this matches what the Bible teaches is possible with False Visions caused by Fallen angels.

Once an abductee, Kathy is now a former abductee, and a Christian, whose experiences have been terminated from happening in her life, by the name and authority of Jesus Christ.

The next case is of Maureen:
"Arriving at the nominated spot, all 3 people then sat in Maureen's car. She saw the same "man" had appeared just outside the vehicle. Neither of the other 2, Judith Magee or Paul Norman, could see anything unusual present. Maureen says that the "man" was beckoning her to join him outside the vehicle. She refused to get out of the car.

Suddenly, according to the others present, Maureen "fainted". She began a verbal description to them whilst she was in this apparent state of unconsciousness. She related she was in a round room somewhere, which was lit, but there was no visible source of illumination. This scene was indistinguishable from the consensus reality that we call "real life".

The "man" just appeared in the room, in which there was also a mushroom shaped object rising up from the floor. This was stemmed, with a broad domed top. There appeared to be an inner hemisphere, wobbling around, and it was covered with what looked to be hieroglyphics on it. The "man" told her to describe what she could see, and this she did, to be heard by the 2 in the car. She could see no doors, or windows in this room, and so began to be scared. She started to cry, then woke, still in the car, with tears in her eyes, saying she could not remember anything that had just occurred. The 2 in the car filled her in on what had transpired."
-Keith Basterfield, "Maureen Puddy: An Australian Abductee Physically Present During An Abduction", 1992, As presented at the 1992 Abduction Study Conference at M.I.T

Two different aspects of False Visions are distinctly represented here. The first, like that of Kathy, was a partial overlaying onto objective reality in a waking state. However, unlike Kathy's case in which all the people saw the UFO, in this case only Maureen saw the entity outside the car, while two people with her did not see it. Maureen alone was having a False Vision, while those with her were not. I would like to point out the same pattern occurs with "ghost encounters" in which someone with supposedly "special sight or powers" can see the ghosts but others with them cannot.

The second False Vision seen here was a full overlaying of objective reality, in a trance state. This is very similar to the case of Robert. The experiences were real to the bodily senses for Maureen, and she seemed to be somewhere else. But in this case Maureen was speaking to people with her while in the trance state, and in her case the passage of time seemed normal. Although she perceived herself in her body in another location in a way that felt real to all of her bodily senses, she never left the car and the two people with her. Maureen also spoke out loud to the people with her during this False Vision experience.

The next case may be of an extreme case of time perception manipulation, or there may be some other explanation for the experience. But we are going to cover this case assuming the time perception manipulation is factual as is recounted with insistence by the abductee. And time perception manipulation as we have covered occurs in False Visions. "The Mars Records" and "The Mars Records 2" detail probably the most extreme case of time perception manipulation I have read about in a False Vision, which is said to have lasted for a subjective period of 20 years. The entirety of the books by Stephanie Relfe, is about the experiences of her husband Michael, with many details.

To summarize, Michael was a childhood abductee, who in the 70s enlisted in the US military. In 1976 Michael had a very unusual experience. He remembered enlisting in a special military program. He then experienced traveling through a "portal" to Mars.

He experienced what seemed to be 20 years of time, which he spent on Mars, and afterwards he perceived his body was made younger and he perceived he traveled back through the "portal" to 1976. Then he was back on Earth, and the time was about a week after he remembers leaving to Mars. During those perceived 20 years he remembers being stationed on the planet Mars on a US military base, working in a Top Secret military operation. He remembers having a wife on Mars, who died on Mars. There were many aliens throughout his experiences, Grays and Reptilians, as well as a Martian population of millions of human people.

In several incidents in the books, the fallen angels include in the False vision a piece of technology, a "portal", which is portrayed as a time travel machine. As seen in other cases, time can seem to be gained subjectively during abductions, in time perception manipulation. However, in the case of Robert mentioned earlier, while he experienced hours during a minute, his body did not actually go anywhere. This is known as a witness remained with his body for those objective minutes during his subjectively hours-long experiences. As such, actual physical time travel did not take place in either of these cases, but rather the False Vision enabled subjective time perception manipulation.

I would describe this 20-year experience of Michael as a False Vision, of extreme subjective duration in time perception manipulation. Other experiences in the book seem to involve Physical manifestation along with the False Visions.

It is important to note that sometimes fallen angels do cause abductees to see "humans" during a False Vision; however these are not real humans, but instead are part of the vision caused by the fallen angel (exceptions being cases of a group of people attacked together by fallen angels).

In many cases in which fallen angels cause False Visions of humans, the humans are military personnel, and advanced technology appears to be present, these kinds of abductions are called "Mil-abs" for "military abductions". Except in rare cases of actual government investigation of abductions and interviews with abductees, these Mi-labs are caused by fallen angels, and are just a subset variety of more typical "alien abduction" experiences. The entire experience, like other False visions, is a vision, including the military personnel and advanced technology the person sees.

Remember, these experiences are real to the bodily senses, and the perception of time passage seems normal to the abductee during the experience. Fallen angels sometimes do display technology in False visions, technology which (deceptively) seems to work time travel, which adds a new layer of confusion for the abductee. Fallen angels have expansive supernatural abilities, which they were originally created with by God, and the technology seen is just part of the False vision, which is a deception.

About 2 years after this 20-subjective-year False vision of Mars, in the late 1970s, Michael became a Christian. In the book he gives God and the Lord Jesus Christ credit for his deliverance from the enemy.

"This book is dedicated to God and the Lord Jesus Christ, for without them this book would never have been written… I want to thank the LORD JESUS CHRIST, my saviour for His mercy and blessings and for removing me from the hands of the enemy. It is only by His love and grace that I am on the road to recovery from the effects of mind control and manipulation…

"I also know that the enemy cannot do anything to me unless God allows it and that God has given me weapons to fight back (see the section on deliverance). I will use those weapons without hesitation…

"I believe that only God has the answer for what is happening to the world at this times and that spiritual warfare is a vital part of His ministry for these end times. It is clear that spiritual warfare and deliverance is the only thing that has not been used against these projects and that God's weapons are superior to the weapons of the enemy."
-The Mars Records, www.metatech.org Dedication, Thank You pgs. 262

According to their website, Michael and Stephanie Relfe, both abductees, have been completely free from abductions for over 7 years now. They say this is from using spiritual warfare and deliverance methods, and through the name and authority of the Lord Jesus Christ.

In reference to being set free from abductions, Michael writes in The Mars Records 2, pg. 205: "You can do the exact same things as I have if you have a personal relationship with The Lord Jesus Christ and if you have faith and follow the warfare prayers in this document. Prayer does not rely on metaphysical abilities or training. I myself do NOTHING. God performs the miracles."

So far we have covered a variety of False visions, but the next case of Howard, from CE4 Research Group, is one of terrifying dreams.

"…I was not a Christian at this time either. The next experiences I had with the Greys was several years after that when they decided to 'contact' me personally. I remember having a strange dream about them; it wasn't anything bad but just strange, strange enough for me to remember it. I remember laughing about it to someone I knew. The very next night was absolutely terrifying and it left me in no doubt that I was under attack. In my dream I was running away from a UFO and it kept swooping down and buzzing me with its energy. Its energy was one of indescribable terror and malevolence.
Anyway the next day I was quite alarmed because I knew these weren't just dreams and that I was dealing with something quite evil and dangerous. Things got worse and worse because they kept at me every night. It got to the point where I became too afraid to go to sleep because I knew they were waiting for me. Have you ever seen the film nightmare on Elm Street? Well I was living that. I do remember in my dreams that I used violence on them, but this did not harm them not even in the slightest. To be honest with you, I think they quite enjoyed it; it was like a game for them. I was getting extremely desperate; I couldn't work or think because I was too afraid to sleep so I was tired all the time."
-CE4 Research Group, the Testimony of Howard,
www.alienresistance.org/ce4testimonies.htm

This case described UFOs and "gray aliens" appearing in nightmares, which were so terrible they were causing him to be afraid to go to sleep. This is like the terrifying dreams and visions Job describes in the Bible, which he experienced while under attacks from Satan.

Howard later describes turning to the Bible for answers, and soon being set free from having these dreams which were destroying his life. He credits Jesus Christ and God with having freed him from these dreams.

Chapter 6 - Alien Abduction Experiences
Physical Manifestations

I am only going to be including one case example of the Physical Manifestation of a fallen angel, known as the Malmstrom UFO Incident. I think many Physical manifestations do take place today, in minor ways. Many of these could arguably be found on TV shows such as "Ghost Hunters" and similar paranormal shows, which record "voices of ghosts", and things like that. Also, there are supposedly many real photos or videos of orbs, ghosts, and even UFOs and aliens on the internet. This seems to be physical manifestation, perhaps directly onto film. And this is besides the injuries which abductees get during False Vision experiences. These all seem to be minor physical manifestations which go along with False Vision experiences. But I am only going to be including one case of physical manifestation, which seems to be a major incident, and shows more of the extreme line that fallen angels seem to be crossing today.

There are many declassified military reports, documenting military encounters with UFOs. I hope these have a level of credibility that is acceptable. I only am personally aware of one such documented military reporting that fits the supernatural requirements to clearly show it was a Physical Manifestation of fallen angels. This is due to a supernaturally caused electronic malfunction that is otherwise unexplainable.

March 16, 1967
"Early in the morning on the sixteenth, at Malmstrom AFB in Montana, one of the most extraordinary events in the history of military-UFO encounters took place. Under a clear and dark Montana sky, an airman with the Oscar Flight Launch Control Center (LCC) saw a starlike object zigzagging high above him. Soon, a larger and closer light also appeared and acted in similar fashion. He called his NCO, and the two men watched inawe as the lights streaked through the sky, maneuvering in impossible ways. The NCO phoned his commander, Robert Salas, who was below ground in the launch control center. Salas was dubious. "Great," he said. "You just keep watching them and let me know if they get any closer."

A few minutes later, the NCO called Salas again. As Salas later wrote, this time he was clearly frightened and shouted that a red, glowing UFO was hovering outside the front gate. "What do you want us to do?" asked the NCO. Salas told him to make sure the site was secure while he phoned the command post. "Sir," replied the NCO, "I have to go now, one of the guys just got injured." Before Salas could ask about the injury, the NCO was off the line. The man, who was not seriously injured, was evacuated by helicopter to the base. Meanwhile, Salas woke his commander, Lt. Fred Meiwald. As he briefed Meiwald, an alarm rang through the small capsule, and both men saw a "No-Go" light turn on for one of the missiles. Within seconds, several more missiles went down in succession.

Twenty miles away, at the Echo-Flight launch facilities, the same scenario was taking place. First Lt. Walter Figel, the deputy crew commander of the Missile Combat Crew, was at his station when one of the Minuteman missiles went into "No-Go" status. He immediately called the missile site to determine the cause of the problem. Was it because of the scheduled missile maintenance, he asked the security guard? No, came the response, as the maintenance had not yet taken place. However, continued the guard, a UFO had been hovering over the site. Like Salas, Figel doubted the story. Before he had any time to reflect on this, however, ten more ICBMs in rapid succession reported a "No-Go" condition. Within seconds, the entire flight was down.

Strike teams were dispatched to two of the E-flight launch facilities, where maintenance crews were already at work. Figel had not told the strike teams about the UFO report. Upon their arrival, however, the teams reported back to him that all of the maintenance and security personnel had been watching UFOs hover over each of the sites.

The missiles were down for the greater part of a day. The air force investigation included full-scale tests on-site, as well as laboratory tests at the Boeing Company's Seattle plant. No cause for the shutdown could be found. The Boeing engineering chief said, "there was no technical explanation that could explain the event."
-Richard M. Dolan, UFOs and the National Security State, Pgs. 322-323

In the Malmstrom UFO incident, UFOs are associated with the supernatural electronic malfunction of at least 15 nuclear ICBMs. Scientists and engineers examined what had happened, and concluded "there was no technical explanation that could explain the event". As such I would say these UFOs were caused by a fallen angel causing a large group to have a False Vision of the form of a UFO. But at the same time, fallen angels also physically manifested, so as to cause supernatural electronic malfunctions to several nuclear missiles in the immediate vicinity. This technological malfunction is a more major documented event of physical manifestation of fallen angels, which left behind documented military records as evidence that this event occurred, as well as some military personnel who claim to have witnessed this event.

Chapter 7 - Alien Abduction Experiences
False Visions Combined with Partial Physical Manifestation

The next cases of Fallen Angelic Attacks are of False Visions which are combined with Partial Physical Manifestation.

The Valdes Case

"On April 25, 1977, Valdés, along with five members of an army patrol, saw two bright objects descending from the sky. Valdés set out alone to investigate and, according to the men, simply vanished. Fifteen minutes later, they said, he reappeared, tried to speak and passed out. The date on his watch had been advanced five days, and he had about a week's growth of beard."
-Cate Setterfield, Armed Forces Reveal UFO Presence in Chile, The Valparaiso Times 2/11/07

"The corporal moved toward the object. He disappeared for some 15 minutes. When he reappeared, he was shaking and his voice seemed different. The light had been illuminating the whole area...He then became unconscious and was attended by his fellow men till he awoke some two hours later. The UFO also disappeared about this time. While the unconscious Corporal Valdes was assisted by his patrol, his men made another strange observation. They saw that Valdes had a beard growth equivalent to several days without shaving. He had been well shaven before the incident. As Valdes awoke he exclaimed, "I don't remember anything from the moment I left you." He then ordered, "Get ready to leave because it's 4:30 in the morning. It was actually about 7 AM. His calendar watch had stopped at 4:30 but the date was five days advanced - to the 30th instead of the 25th."
-Aerial Phenomena Research Organization (APRO), 1977

Much like the Biblical account of Jesus tempted by Satan seen in Luke 4, in which Jesus experienced a far longer period of time in less than a second, the Valdes case shows time perception manipulation. In principle, this is the same thing.

In the Valdes case, the time manipulation seems very physical instead of perceptual, because his watch was moved ahead by 5 days, and he had 5 days growth of a beard, after only 15 minutes of time passing in objective reality. It also seems very physical because he disappeared for 15 minutes and his men could not see him. As such, this seems to be a case of a False Vision couple with powerful Physical Manifestation seen in the effects on Valdes' body.

One way to look at this is that, like the boils of Job described in Biblical Physical Manifestations onto the body, a fallen angel was able to supernaturally cause rapid hair growth, and also alter Valdes' watch. The men might have been blocked with a group False Vision, from being able to see Valdes, even if he was nearby within normal sight distance. This is similar to the case of Peter escaping from prison in that no one could see him. There is nothing in this case that necessitates that Valdez went anywhere, merely that those with him could no longer see him. And there is nothing here that proves his body experienced 5 days worth of time in 15 minutes, but the simplest explanation would be that fallen angels affected his body supernaturally to grow hair very quickly, and altered his watch.

And so there is nothing in this case which "must" indicate the science fiction concept of "time travel". Nothing in this case shows that Valdes traveled backwards in time, or that he traveled forward in time more than anyone else did (that being 15 minutes). Valdes' experiences during the abduction are unknown, but even if he had reported he subjectively experienced 5 days worth of time in 15 minutes, this would have been time perception manipulation in a False Vision. This is a separate matter from the hair growth, and his watch changing, and other people not being able to see him. The simplest explanation is that this entire event was staged with the goal in mind of deception, it being caused by fallen angels whose goal is to deceive.

In a cases like this one, and as in the case of Michael Relfe, it becomes apparent that fallen angels want people to believe that they can time travel – which in itself is a good reason to not believe such – but there are alternate explanations for everything which occurred in this case which match Biblical teaching on what fallen angels are known to be able to do. However, there is nothing in the Bible which teaches that angels can time travel, and in opposition, the Bible does teach that God has absolute authority over time, and appoints things to happen at certain times, which fallen angels cannot interfere with, or alter. Jesus Christ is "the alpha and omega, the beginning and the end".

The next case of Anita is a good overview of physical injuries that many abductees have after fallen angelic attacks:

"Anita has been consciously aware of UFO activity since childhood, and her brothers and sisters have also had recurrent UFO events throughout their lives. So, perhaps, may have some of Anita's children and grandchildren...
So are the **various marks and injuries she has discovered on her body.** "Lots of mornings," Anita said, "I have gotten up **feeling like someone beat me up in my sleep.**" This is another common abductee report, waking up with sore, damaged-feeling muscles and joints. "**I have waked up with bruises on my arms, shoulders, and legs,**" she continued, "with no idea where they came from. I have **found scratches that I could not remember having gotten the day before.**"
The evidence for vigorous physical activity during the night, although unremembered, comes from more than just Anita's sore or scarred body, however. In one incident, she woke up in the morning and felt an unfamiliar pain in her right hand. "I sat up in bed," she explained, "and found that **sometime during the night my ring had been squashed on my finger.**" She managed with effort to remove the ring, but **neither her husband nor a jeweler could completely restore its original shape.**
On another occasion, Anita **got out of bed one morning and found the crucifix from her necklace lying on the floor.** "It had been on my neck the night before," she said, "and the chain was still on [me]. But the only way to remove the crucifix is to remove the necklace and take it off the chain."
She has also awakened several mornings to discover that something had happened to her clothing, a report frequently

echoed by other abductees. In one instance, **she woke up with her nightie on backward**, although she was certain she had not taken it off, turned it around, and put it back on. And on a different occasion she found that **the nightie was not only backward but had also been turned inside-out**. In the night during one of these events, she had an altered-state experience in which she recalled a group of Tan aliens observing her as she was "free-falling," an event which did not feel unduly upsetting for some reason....
Anita had quite a severe reaction to another similar event, however, venting much more emotion than the situation seemed to call for. It was in the winter, during the Christmas holidays one night, and she had **worn socks to bed** for extra warmth. When she woke up the next day and **found that one of her socks was missing**,...Anita was also physically upset that morning, **suffering from a violent headache and nausea which caused her to vomit, yet there was no illness to account for the symptoms.** Still, she might not have been overly concerned about the vanished sock and her physical problems, if her young granddaughter hadn't made a disturbing comment...The **seven-year-old child told her grandmother that some "mean men" had come in and taken her away during the night**. When Anita asked her to describe the "mean men," **the little girl called them "the mushroom men."** "What are the mushroom men?" Anita asked, and her granddaughter then found the book MISSING TIME by Budd Hopkins and pointed to the drawing on the cover.
...The girl said the creatures were about a foot tall, gray-skinned and had four fingers rather than five-a detail not apparent in the cover picture. There were quite a few of these entities present, she said. Anita remembered nothing strange that night herself, but the physical symptoms, the missing sock, and her granddaughter's story were indicative enough of an intrusive incident to be of great concern."
-Karla Turner PhD, Taken: Inside the Alien-Human Abduction Agenda, Pgs. 46, 50-51

As for Physical Manifestation, there were physical aftereffects that remained and were seen by others, such as her bent ring. The case of Anita is a good overview of physical injuries that many abductees have after this type of fallen angelic attack.

In this case there was another person involved, her 7 year old granddaughter that saw part of the experience, and this part was a case of a False Vision seen by multiple people. As in the Valdes case, part of the False Vision on the child was her grandmother seemed to be missing, in that she was unseen and not visible for a period of time. And the child in the False Vision also saw her grandmother be taken, deceiving her into thinking her grandmother has went somewhere. But the simplest explanation is that Anita did not go anywhere, but that her and her granddaughter both experienced False Visions that night. And this along with various degrees of Physical manifestation throughout Anita's experiences, including objects moved, and injuries, and physical illness.

It is important to note that innocent children can be attacked by fallen angels, as in this case, and this is a type of generational curse. While on that topic, another case from Karla Turner's book Taken is of a child (though this case does not involve Physical manifestation):

"When I was seven or eight years old," Beth related, "my father gave us permission, my sister and me, to go outside and play with the other children, who were playing hide-and-seek. It was close to six in the evening. I remember that I went to hide between some bushes, and then I heard a sound, somebody else. And as I turned, I saw what I thought at that moment was one of the other kids. "The next thing I know," she continued, "it was dark, and I was very surprised. When I got home, my father was very mad at me and my mother was very upset. My father told me that they had been calling me and looking for me for hours. But I couldn't understand it," she said. "The place where I was hiding was less than a hundred feet from the front of the house. I was hiding there, and it was daylight, and then the next thing I know it was dark- and I was scared.
"Recently I had another memory about that," she added. "That kid I thought was there, he was an alien, one of the Grays. He took me to a ship, but I don't remember what happened after that."
-Karla Turner PhD, Taken: Inside the Alien-Human Abduction Agenda, Pg. 56

I think the most efficient way to explain this case is that first the child Beth had a False Vision of an "alien" approaching her, which overlaid onto objective reality. Then Beth was effectively hidden from her parents by fallen angels by a False Vision her parents were caused to have, which kept them from seeing their daughter as they looked for her. While this was going on, the child Beth experienced a False Vision of being with Grays on a ship. A combination of various aspects of False Visions would suffice to explain this experience.

This case is somewhat reminiscent of the abduction case of Travis Walton, who was missing for 5 days, and remembered only 2 hours. I do feel that the explanation for the case of Beth is also an adequate explanation for the Walton case. He was present, but all those involved in searching for him were prevented from seeing him. The main difference is that he was made unconscious for the majority of the 5 days, except for the 2 hours in which he experienced a False Vision.

Chapter 8 - Modern Physics and the Abilities of Fallen Angels False Visions, Dreams, and Physical Manifestation

And so after looking at several "alien abduction" cases it seems that the abilities of Fallen angels to cause False Visions (and all that entails) and terrifying dreams, as well as elements of Physical manifestation, are sufficient to explain what abductees experience.

Next we are going to move on to looking at the Physics and Science of this being the case, and how science does not conflict with the existence of fallen angels, or them having these abilities. Some people think that the most straightforward explanation for these alien abductions is flesh-and-blood extraterrestrials with advanced technology, even perhaps having time-travel capabilities, and perhaps with military involvement. And to some people, the explanation of fallen angels with vast supernatural powers who can cause powerful deceptions seems too spiritual of an answer. But the understanding of Modern science and it's theories actually allows both for the existence of such creatures as fallen angels, and for them to have inherit supernatural powers such as these. The explanation of fallen angels is not any less science-friendly than biological extraterrestrials with advanced technology, and actually in some ways the explanation of fallen angels is more science-friendly, contradicting modern known science far less than the biological ET with advanced technology explanation.

Some people think the miraculous is impossible, and use science as a justification for this claim. The miraculous could be miracles from God, or worked through Holy angels. Or the miraculous can come in the form of false signs, miracles and wonders from fallen angels, such as what they do in causing False Visions, dreams, and physical manifestations.

The goal of the following is to show the miraculous abilities of God, Holy and fallen angels are allowed by science, using modern physics terminology and theories. This is towards being about to explain how they might do such things, from a modern physics perspective.

The main point of doing this is to show that modern science does not preclude the existence of the miraculous. I believe modern science actually completely allows for either God or angels of either kind to work miracles without violating the laws of science, and for the existence of angels and their Biblically described abilities. The science involved is all just theoretical, mainly secular theories, and I do not claim any of it is correct, though much of it is accepted as such by some people.

How the Miraculous Does Not Conflict with Modern Science Theories

All of the categories of angelic Visions would be called supernatural events.

There are some words in the Bible to describe the "supernatural" activities of God, Holy angels, and fallen angels.

Greek - signs "semeion" (4592), wonders "teras" (5059), and miracles "dynamis" (1411).

These same 3 words are all used in the context of:

1. God - the power of God in signs, wonders, and miracles that God, Jesus Christ, and the Holy Spirit through the gift of miracles, as seen throughout the Bible

2. Holy Angels - Holy angels. (Acts 2:22, 5:12, 2 Peter 2:11, Heb 2:4)

3. Fallen angels, of the dragon and beast, and the "3 evil spirits like frogs". (Matt 24:24, 2 Thes 2:9, Rev 13:2, 14, 16:14)

From the Bible it is clear that God in His three persons, Holy angels, and also Fallen angels, are all capable of performing signs, wonders, and miracles. How, in physics terminology, might God work signs, wonders, and miracles?

Gen 1:1 **In the beginning** God created the heavens and the earth.

Eph 3:18 May be able to comprehend with all saints what [is] the **breadth**, and **length**, and **depth**, and **height**

Rev 1:8 **I am** Alpha and Omega, **the beginning and the ending, saith the Lord**, which is, and which was, and which is to come, the Almighty.

According to modern science, we live in an observably 4 dimensional universe. The universe is made of space(3) + and time(1) dimensions, which equal the Spacetime we can see. God made all the 3 dimensions of space that we see (length, width, and height), when God "created the heavens and the earth". (Eph 3:18 also references to the "depth" which compares more the size or extent or full scope of something.) God made the dimension of time "in the beginning", which marked the creation of time itself, the dimension of time as we know it. God is eternal, and having made time itself, God is outside of time, and was here before time was created. God has complete authority and control over the dimension of time. God also made the three dimensions of space that we can see, and is also outside of them. So, God made it all, and is outside of the entire universe, having created it.

Above I use the term "dimension" as it is referred to in science. To quote Wikipedia,

"In physical terms, dimension refers to the constituent structure of all space (cf. volume) and its position in time (perceived as a scalar dimension along the t-axis), as well as the spatial constitution of objects within — structures that have correlations with both particle and field conceptions, interact according to relative properties of mass, and which are fundamentally mathematical in description. These or other axes may be referenced to uniquely identify a point or structure in its attitude and relationship to other objects and events. Physical theories that incorporate time, such as general relativity, are said to work in 4-dimensional "space-time", (defined as a Minkowski space). Modern theories tend to be "higher-dimensional" including quantum field and string theories. The state-space of quantum mechanics is an infinite-dimensional function space." – Dimension, Wikipedia

This use of the term "dimension" should not be confused with the science fiction concept of a "parallel universe". Again to quote Wikipedia on the term "Dimension",
"Science fiction texts often mention the concept of dimension, when really referring to parallel universes, alternate universes, or other planes of existence. This usage is derived from the idea that to travel to parallel/alternate universes/planes of existence one must travel in a direction/dimension besides the standard ones. In effect, the other universes/planes are just a small distance away from our own, but the distance is in a fourth (or higher) spatial (or non-spatial) dimension, not the standard ones."

The "parallel universe" concept in science fiction actually is very different from the use of the term "dimension" in science, as you can see above. In theory, a "parallel universe" would also have 3 spatial dimensions (length, width, height) and a time dimension. That means a "parallel universe" in theory actually has 4 dimensions of its own. Additionally the assumption is that there is a 5th dimension to our universe which would be used to allow travel to the parallel world, which has its own 4 dimensions.
It would not be accurate to say a "parallel universe" uses the same 4 dimensions that our universe has, because by definition a "universe" is everything that is. So a "parallel universe" would have to have its own construct of dimensions which define its reality and cosmological structure, and not just borrow use of the dimensions inherit in our own universe. This is of course all fictional theories that come from science fiction, which has nothing to do with actual science. And I want to clarify this, as any statement that science has straight theories on "other dimensions" does NOT have anything to do with the science fiction concept of "parallel universes". If science were to find some evidence of observation of a "5th dimension" inherent in our universe, this has nothing to do with a "parallel universe". The term "dimension" is a science term first, and has been misleadingly borrowed by science fiction in such a way that its meaning is construed.

The Bible teaches that "in the beginning" God made the "heavens and the earth", and that at the end of the 6th day God "saw every thing that He had made, and, behold, [it was] very good...Thus the heavens and the earth were finished, and all the host of them." Gen 1:31,2:1.

This means that in making the heavens and the earth, and the host of them, God made everything that He made. There isn't anything else besides what God made, and there is no mention made of any other universe besides the entirety of the universe we know which God made. So there actually are no "parallel universes" and the concept itself contradicts the Bible, as this universe is all God is said to have made, and is well-defined by the Bible. God made the heavens and the earth, and these terms are well-defined, and there is nothing more that God made besides the heavens and the Earth, and the host of them.

We know what the Earth is, but beyond this there are multiple heaven(s) that God made, and the Bible defines each of them for us.

The first heaven is the sky or atmosphere, and is where the rain comes from and where the birds fly. (Gen 1:7-8, Jer 4:25, Rev 19:17, Deut 11:17, 28:12, Jud 5:4, Acts 14:17)

The second heaven is outer-space, where the sun and moon, and all the stars, planets, and galaxies are located. (Jer 8:2, Isa 13:10)

The third heaven is where God dwells, where God's throne is, and this is where the angels are who are in heaven. (1 Kin 8:30, Psa 2:4, 11:4, Isa 66:1, 2 Ch 18:18, Matt 5:16) The third heaven is also called the "highest heaven" or the "heaven of heavens". It is called the "heaven of heavens" because it is the heaven of the first and second heavens. (1 Kin 8:27, Deut 10:14)

And so the Earth, the atmosphere (first heaven), outer-space (second heaven), and where God's throne and the angels in heaven dwell (third heaven) is all the areas that exist in all of God's creation. None of these are a "parallel universe", and so the Bible does not describe any "parallel universes" to exist. Rather, the Bible's thorough defining of the entirety of creation actually precludes the existence of anything along the lines of the concept of a "parallel universe".

All that being said, using the term "dimensions" in a science context, (spatial length, width, height, and time) are there more dimensions that God made, besides the 4 we can perceive, and see with the naked eye?

It seems possible that there are more dimensions than we can perceive, because the Bible teaches there is an invisible spiritual realm.

The Earth has 4 dimensions that we can see, but also the Bible teaches that there is an invisible spiritual realm all around us on Earth, and in this spiritual realm, spirits have a presence, like Holy angels, fallen angels, and demons. We know that demons, when they are cast out, travel through desert places, yet we cannot see them. (Matt 12:43, Luke 11:24) We know that an army can exist on this Earth invisibly, right in front of us, while remaining unseen. This happened in the case of Elisha and his friend,

"And Elisha prayed, and said, LORD, I pray thee, open his eyes, that he may see. And the LORD opened the eyes of the young man; and he saw: and, behold, the mountain [was] full of horses and chariots of fire round about Elisha." (2 Kin 6:17)

When God opened his eyes to the spiritual realm, he saw an army all around them fighting for them. This is the spiritual realm that exists all around us, but is invisible. The same sort of army, God's army which is the "host of heaven" or the angels of God, is mentioned in Josh 5-6 in the battle of Jericho.

"And he said, Nay; but [as] captain of the host of the LORD am I now come. And Joshua fell on his face to the earth, and did worship, and said unto him, What saith my lord unto his servant?" (Josh 5:14)

The "host" of the Lord is His army, which are the angels. While the walls of Jericho seemed to fall miraculously, the Bible does indicate that the army of God's angels was present. It is entirely likely that God's angels had a hand in the actual mechanics of the wall of Jericho coming down. And so we know there is an invisible spiritual realm here on Earth.

In the first heaven, the atmosphere, the Bible also indicates that besides the physical part of the atmosphere, of air and clouds, that the invisible spiritual realm is there also. Angels fly in the atmosphere, which is the first heaven, so the invisible spiritual realm must be there too. (Eze 8:3, John 1:32, Rev 8:13) And Satan is called the "prince of the power of the air" by the Bible, and "air" refers to the atmosphere (Eph 2:2).

The third heaven seems to be entirely made of an invisible spiritual realm, as when we look into the farthest reaches of space, we cannot see God's throne or the angels. As obvious as that is, it shows us that precisely wherever God's throne and the angels of heaven are, they are in an invisible spiritual realm. And this makes sense that the third heaven is a spiritual realm, as the third heaven is where God is, and God is spirit.

In between is the second heaven, which is defined by the Bible as outer-space. The Bible clearly indicates that the second heaven also contains the invisible spiritual realm, and that angels pass through it as they descend to Earth, and ascend back to the third heaven.

"And he dreamed, and behold a ladder set up on the earth, and the top of it reached to heaven: and behold the angels of God ascending and descending on it. And, behold, the LORD stood above it, and said, I [am] the LORD God of Abraham thy father, and the God of Isaac: the land whereon thou liest, to thee will I give it, and to thy seed…"

Gen 28:12-13 makes clear that the second heaven, which is outer-space, must also contain the invisible spiritual realm, as we do not see the angels as they ascend and descend through the second heaven. The ladder which Jacob saw indicates God has given the angels a method by which to ascend and descend. That Jacob could see Lord above the ladder indicates that the distance was not very far that the angels had to travel. So the Bible seems to teach that the angels do not actually have to transverse the vast distances of outer-space in order to reach the earth, as is seen in the physical dimensions. Rather, in the invisible spiritual realm, the distance is short enough between heaven and earth, no longer than a ladder you can see the top of. Like a sort of permanent ladder has been created by God for angels to travel through the 2nd heaven, going between the 1st and 3rd heavens. And so angels can be dispatched to Earth quickly, as the invisible spiritual realm is not limited by the way time is bounded in physics by the physical dimensions. How this actually works is somewhat vague, but we can get the general idea from what the Bible does say. In any case, the invisible spiritual realm also seems to exist throughout the second heaven, which is outer-space.

And so the Earth and all 3 of the heavens have an invisible spiritual realm that seems to pervade through all of them. Here on Earth the spiritual realm is all around us, but invisible. The Bible teaches that God created an invisible side to the universe,

"For by him all things were created: things in heaven and on earth, visible and invisible, whether thrones or powers or rulers or authorities; all things were created by him and for him." (Col 1:16)

And it should be noted that the terms here for "rulers, authorities" all refer to fallen angels. This can be seen by comparing this with Eph 6:12,
"For we wrestle not against flesh and blood, but against principalities, against powers, against the rulers of the darkness of this world, against spiritual wickedness in high [places]."
And so these powers and authorities are the invisible fallen angels.

While they can physically manifest, it seems that fallen angels also have something akin to bodies made of spirit. We are 4 dimensional in our physicality, being made for 4 dimensions. Angels are spirits, and Jesus said after His Resurrection in Luke 24:

"Behold my hands and my feet, that it is I myself: handle me, and see; for a spirit hath not flesh and bones, as ye see me have."
Luke 24:39

This could be taken, that truly angels are not physical life of the 3 physical dimensions we live in, as we are. Rather, angels are spirits of the spiritual realm, and their "bodies" exist in the spiritual realm. It would make sense that their bodies are composed of the substance of this invisible spiritual realm they live in, as human bodies are composed of the stuff of the 3 physical dimensions we live in.

1 Cor 15:40, 44 [There are] also celestial bodies, and bodies terrestrial: but the glory of the celestial [is] one, and the [glory] of the terrestrial [is] another… It is sown a natural body; it is raised a spiritual body. There is a natural body, and there is a spiritual body.

The Bible acknowledges that there can be bodies made of spirit, or spiritual bodies. As our human terrestrial bodies are composed of 4-dimensional physical matter, it would make sense that living spirit or heavenly bodies would be composed of the equivalent of the "matter" of the invisible spiritual realm. Angels have such spiritual bodies, and were created with such. It would make sense that there is at least a 5th dimension, if not more, and that the angels' bodies are composed of the analogy to our "4d matter" which is in that spiritual realm. The spiritual realm might be composed of several dimensions, in the scientific sense of the term, such as a spiritual realm width, length, and height. But even if the spiritual realm is just 1 extra dimension, in the scientific sense of the term, the invisible spiritual realm would still be a 5th dimension, 1 more dimension that the 4 dimensional physical world which we routinely perceive.

All of this leads to the point that this invisible spiritual realm may be composed of more dimensions, as per the scientific use of the term. The additional dimension(s) of the invisible spiritual realm, would be an extra dimension that is at least one more than the 4 dimensions that we perceive. Thus it would be fair to call angels "extra-dimensional", meaning of more dimensions than us, esp. if the invisible spiritual realm correlates to extra dimensions, per the science use of the term.

However, God is **not** simply extra-dimensional. God is eternal, and therefore is what I call "outer-dimensional". God is outside of dimensionality, being eternal and the Creator of everything that is, including all theoretical dimensions of the heavens and earth, and everything living in them. So to coin a term, God is "outer-dimensional". This is an important distinction between the God the Creator, and His creation. The Bible says that all three of the heavens and the earth cannot contain God, which makes sense as He made them all; however they do manage to contain everything He created.

"But will God indeed dwell on the earth? behold, the heaven and heaven of heavens cannot contain thee; how much less this house that I have builded?" 1 Kin 8:27

Now, the Earth is made by God, and it has visible dimensions that science has studied many things in, and the same for the first and second heaven. We also know there is an invisible spiritual realm throughout God's creation. Science has said much on the visible physical realm. But the fact that the spiritual realm is invisible does not mean that science will never have anything to say about it, or that no rules or bounds may operate upon the angels who live there. In fact, it seems that there are rules and bounds, like laws of physics, which are inherit in the spiritual realm as well. Even the battle in Rev 12 between the Holy angels and the fallen angels indicates that there are opposing forces best described as some spiritual realm physics being present. This is implied even in that the Holy angels prevailed, and pushed the fallen angels out of heaven, casting them down to earth. You can't have one angel pushing another without some concept of physics being implied, even in the spiritual realm. As such, there is some chance that the invisible spiritual realm does have physics rules under which it operates, and if so, that where the invisible spiritual realm touches the visible physical realm that we know, science might be able to glean some insight, or give some insight. This possibility is especially interesting in light of more and more of modern physics studying things which are invisible, and theories on what invisible dimensions may exist behind the scenes in the universe.

So if we were to guess that the invisible spiritual realm, and the creatures who are there, do have something to do with an extra dimension or dimensions (in the scientific use of the term), and spirits are therefore extra-dimensional beings, what would modern physics have to say about this?

Modern physics actually does include the topic of extra dimensions, and talk from scientists about extra dimensions has to do with something called "string theory" or "superstring theory".

Some branches in modern physics are well established through experiments, such as gravity, relativity, quantum mechanics, much of particle physics, electromagnetism, and the weak and strong nuclear forces. String theory is not established, but rather is an attempt to bring all these branches of the tree of physics together, to connect them, to draw and see the trunk that all the branches stem from. String theory is highly theoretical, unproven, likely improvable and unverifiable, highly mathematical, and requires 10-11 dimensions to theoretically be able to describe the trunk of the tree of modern physics.

Here is quote from Lisa Randall PhD, a leading theoretical physicist and expert on particle physics, string theory, and cosmology:

"How many dimensions of space are there? Do we really know? By now, I hope you would agree that it would be overreaching to claim that we know for certain that extra dimensions do not exist. We see three dimensions of space, but there could be more that we haven't yet detected. You know now that extra dimensions can be hidden either because they are curled up and small, or because spacetime is warped and gravity so concentrated in a small region that even an infinite dimension is invisible. Either way, whether dimensions are compact or localized, spacetime would appear to be four-dimensional everywhere, no matter where you are." -Lisa Randall PhD, Warped Passages: Unraveling the Mysteries of the Universe's Hidden Dimensions, pg. 437

Lisa Randall is saying, according to modern physics, that there may be very large, even infinitely large, invisible dimensions that do exist, although we can only perceive the 4 dimensions of space-time. A 5th large dimension such as this could be the invisible spiritual realm taught in the Bible, which contains angels in their spirit bodies of that dimension.

And here is a quote from Stephen Hawking PhD, one of the most famous scientists and theoretical astrophysicists of our time, commenting his thoughts on Randall's work:

If fact, in order to explain the rate in which stars orbit the center of our galaxy, it seems there must be more mass than is accounted for by matter we observe. This missing mass might arise from some exotic species of particles in our world such as WIMPs (weakly interacting massive particles) or axions (very light elementary particles). **But missing mass could also be evidence of the existence of a shadow world with matter in it...** *Instead of the* **extra dimensions** *ending on a shadow brane, another possibility is that* **they are infinite but highly curved, like a saddle.** *Lisa Randall and Raman Sundrum showed that this kind of curvature would act rather like a second brane: the gravitational influence of an object on the brane would be confined to a small neighborhood of the brane and not spread out to infinity in the extra dimensions. As in the shadow brane model, the gravitational field would have the right long-distance falloff to explain the planetary orbits and lab measurements of the gravitational force, but gravity would vary more rapidly at short distances. There is however an important difference between this Randall-Sundrum model and the shadow brane model. Bodies that move under the influence of gravity will produce gravitational waves, ripples of curvature that travel through spacetime at the speed of light. Like the electromagnetic waves of light, gravitational waves should carry energy, a prediction that has been confirmed by observations of the binary pulsar PSR1913+16. If we indeed live on a brane* **in a spacetime with extra dimensions***, gravitational waves generated by the motion of bodies on the brane would travel off into the other dimensions. If there were a second shadow brane, gravitational waves would be reflected back and trapped between the two branes. On the other hand, if there was only a single brane and the* **extra dimensions** *went on forever, as in the Randall-Sundrum model,*

*gravitational waves could escape altogether and carry away energy from our brane world. This would seem to breach one of the fundamental principles of physics: The Law of Conservation of Energy. The total amount of energy remains the same. However, it appears to be a violation only because our view of what is happening is restricted to the brane. **An angel who could see the extra dimensions would know** that the energy was the same, just more spread out."*
-Stephen Hawking PhD, The Universe in a Nutshell, pgs. 184-192

While giving credence to Randall's statement, basically Hawking says that very large extra-dimensions are possible, and would not violate the known laws of physics. In fact, their existence might help explain some rather large befuddling questions in science that are still unanswered, such as missing mass. As such, science allows for the existence of an invisible spiritual realm, potentially one in which angels are, and the spirit bodies of angels could be composed of the stuff of this extra dimension, this invisible realm.

The branch of physics called quantum mechanics deals with particles which are subatomic (that is smaller than an atom). Quantum mechanics has been well-established through scientific experimentation. Unlike string theory, quantum mechanics is a field of practical experimentation. It is in quantum physics that we find the Heisenberg Uncertainty Principle:

In quantum physics, the Heisenberg uncertainty principle states that certain pairs of physical properties, like position and momentum, cannot both be known to arbitrary precision. That is, the more precisely one property is known, the less precisely the other can be known. It is impossible to measure simultaneously both position and velocity of a microscopic particle with any degree of accuracy or certainty. This is not a statement about the limitations of a researcher's ability to measure particular quantities of a system, but rather about the nature of the system itself and hence it expresses a property of the universe.
-Wikipedia, Uncertainty Principle

This basically means that on a subatomic level, that of electrons, quarks, photons, etc., there seems to be a fundamental principal of randomness. Particles go where they seem to want to go. Particles almost seem to choose what they are doing. However, these choices do form an overall pattern, of statistically calculable probabilities.

One of the most well-known and respectable scientists in recent history, instrumental in the development of quantum mechanics, was Richard Feynman PhD. He worked on the Manhattan project developing the atomic bomb, was a recipient of the Nobel Prize in Physics, and is also known for demonstrating the O-ring defects resulting in the space shuttle Challenger tragedy.

To quote Richard Feynman PhD on the Uncertainty Principle in quantum mechanics:

One might still like to ask: "How does it work? What is the machinery behind the law?" No one has found any machinery behind the law. No one can "explain" any more than we have just "explained." No one will give you any deeper representation of the situation. We have no ideas about a more basic mechanism from which these results can be deduced. We would like to emphasize a very important difference between classical and quantum mechanics. **We have been talking about the probability that an electron will arrive in a given circumstance. We have implied that in our experimental arrangement (or even in the best possible one) it would be impossible to predict exactly what would happen. We can only predict the odds!** *This would mean, if it were true, that physics has given up on the problem of trying to predict exactly what will happen in a definite circumstance. Yes! physics has given up.* **We do not know how to predict what would happen in a given circumstance, and we believe now that it is impossible — that the only thing that can be predicted is the probability of different events.** *It must be recognized that this is a retrenchment in our earlier ideal of understanding nature. It may be a backward step but no one has found a way to avoid it.*
No one has figured a way out of this puzzle. So at the present time we must limit ourselves to computing probabilities. We say "at the present time," but **we suspect very strongly that it is something that will be with us forever — that it is impossible to beat that puzzle — that this is the way nature really is.**
-Richard P. Feynman, PhD, The Feynman Lectures on Physics, Vol. 3, pgs.1-10,1-11

So why is it that at the scale of the tiniest parts of the universe, that there is all this randomness? Why has science given up on precise predictability, and accepted that uncertainty and chance rule the microscopic domain of the most basic and fundamental building blocks of the universe? Why can only probabilities be known?

With the advent of quantum mechanics, we have come to recognize that events cannot be predicted with complete accuracy but that there is always a degree of uncertainty. If one likes, **one could ascribe this randomness to the intervention of God**, *but it would be a very strange kind of intervention: there is no evidence that it is directed toward any purpose. Indeed, if it were, it would by definition not be random. In modern times, we have effectively removed the third possibility above by redefining the goal of science: our aim is to formulate a set of laws that enables us to predict events only up to the limit set by the uncertainty principle.* -Stephen Hawking PhD, The Illustrated Brief History of Time, Pg 224

There is always an element of uncertainty or chance, and this affects the behavior of matter on a small scale in a fundamental way. Einstein was almost singlehandedly responsible for general relativity, and he played an important part in the development of quantum mechanics. His feelings about the matter are summed up in the phrase **"God does not play dice." But all the evidence indicates that God is an inveterate gambler and that He throws the dice on every possible occasion.** -Stephen Hawking PhD, Black Holes and Baby Universes, pg. 70

Regarding quantum physics, Einstein said that "God does not play dice", and Stephen Hawking says, "God throws the dice on every possible occasion". But what does the Bible say on the topic of dice and God?

We may throw the dice, but the LORD determines how they fall. Prov 16:33

Assuming that whether it is us or the universe that throws the dice, it makes no difference, then what the Bible indicates is that God set up the universe to "play dice" on a quantum level, but at the same time, God is the one that determines how those "quantum dice" fall.

By "quantum dice" I am referring to all of the subatomic particles/energies and their activities on the microscopic scale of the quantum level.

However, if the uncertainty principle of quantum physics is correct, then the Bible assures us that God still sets the rules and outcomes for the seeming "randomness" of the "quantum dice". God is in control of the randomness and the probabilities that we see.

Some Christians who are Scientists speak on this very issue:

John Byl has a PhD in Astronomy, is the author of the book "God and Cosmos: A Christian View of Time, Space, and the Universe", and is Professor of Mathematics and Head of the Department of Mathematical Sciences at Trinity Western University.

"W.G. Pollard and, more recently, Nancey Murphy advocate that the apparently random events at the quantum level are all specific, intentional acts of God. God's action at this level is limited in that
(1) He respects the integrity of the entities with which He co-operates (e.g., He doesn't change the electron's mass arbitrarily) and
(2) He restricts His action to produce a world that, for all we can tell, is orderly and law-like.
God is the hidden variable. Murphy asserts that this position is not only theologically preferable to indeterminism, but has the further advantage of consistency with the principle of sufficient reason. Of course, if God is directly responsible for quantum events this entails that these are therefore predictable by God. Hence we are left with a deterministic universe, at least at the quantum level."
"God's sovereignty rules out the possibility of agents acting independently of Him. In particular, quantum mechanics does not imply ontological indeterminism, given that determinist interpretations of quantum mechanics are possible, that non-physical secondary causes cannot be ruled out and that God is the primary cause for all events."
-John Byl PhD, "Indeterminacy, Divine action and Human Freedom"

William Pollard PhD, is a Nuclear Physicist and Episcopal Priest, with a PhD in Physics and Honorary doctorates in science, divinity, law, and humane letters. He is the author of "Chance and

Providence: God's Action in a World Governed by Scientific Law". The entire book is on God operating, instead of "chance", in quantum mechanics.

"In the next chapter I will begin the presentation for your consideration of a quite different approach to this problem which seems to me to offer an entirely adequate solution for it. Under it, as we shall attempt to show, there can emerge again in all of its ancient power the fullness of the Biblical response to the living God who is ever active in the whole of His creation sustaining, providing, judging, and redeeming all things, both in heaven and in earth, in accordance with the mysterious and hidden purposes of His might will. At the same time, however, this is accomplished in such a way that the essential integrity and unity of science, both as it is now and as in principle it may become, is fully preserved."
"To Einstein's famous question expressing his abhorrence of quantum mechanics, "Does God throw dice?" the Judeo-Christian answer is not, as so many have wrongly supposed, a denial, but a very positive affirmative. For only in a world in which the laws of nature govern events in accordance with the casting of dice can a Biblical view of a world whose history is responsive to God's will prevail."
-William Pollard PhD, "Chance and Providence: God's Action in a World Governed by Scientific Law", pg. 35, pg. 97

Nancey Murphy PhD, Theologian, is Professor of Christian Philosophy at the Fuller Theological Seminary. She also serves as an editorial advisor for Theology and Science, Theology Today, and Christianity Today. She is the author of "Divine Action In The Natural Order".

"The second strategy for giving an account of the locus of divine action explores quantum physics and seeks to give an account of God's action throughout the natural and human world by means of action at the quantum level (either alone or in conjunction with top-down action). My proposal is motivated theologically. <u>If God is immanent in and acting in all creatures, then necessarily God is acting at the quantum level.</u> Emphasis on this fact has the advantage of sidestepping the problem of interventionism: the laws of quantum mechanics are only statistical and therefore not subject to violation. If, as most interpreters conclude, events at this level are genuinely indeterminate, then there need be no

competition between divine action and physical causation. It is possible from a theistic perspective to interpret current physics as saying that <u>the natural world is intrinsically incomplete and open to divine action at its most basic level</u>."
-Nancey Murphy PhD, Dive Action In The Natural Order, pg. 131

In other words, God is in control and constantly interacting with the world at a quantum level. Where scientists see randomness and probabilities, they are seeing God determine how the dice fall, all the time, in quantum mechanics. The Bible may also present an argument of God controlling the "quantum dice" in Col 1:16-17, referring to Jesus Christ,

"For by him were all things created, that are in heaven, and that are in earth, visible and invisible, whether [they be] thrones, or dominions, or principalities, or powers: all things were created by him, and for him: And he is before all things, and <u>by him all things consist.</u>"

The word here for "consist" is "synistemi" (4921) and it means, "to consist of or be composed of, to cohere, put together, hold together or band together".

According to subatomic physics, it is the quantum force particles of bosons, and gluons that hold together atoms, and particles like photons and electrons that hold together different atoms. As such, this verse in the Bible could be referring to, that it is by God's control over the "quantum dice" that makes these particles we are composed of to hold together. As such, by His actions all things hold together or "by Him all things consist".

Assuming it is true that God does allow randomness at a quantum level of physics, but also constantly controls the outcome of that randomness, besides "upholding all things", like the universe, "by the word of His power" (Heb 1:3), is there another possible reason for God creating the universe to be this way? Could it relate to miracles, signs and wonders? This could very well be the case.

Not only does quantum physics allow for existing particles that we can observe in experiment to act in random ways, but it also allows for particles and antiparticles (antimatter) to pop in and out of existence, seemingly randomly. These particles usually only exist for a very short time, and are called "virtual particles".

"Down at the very tiniest length scale and trillions of times smaller than atoms, is what is known as the Planck scale where the concept of length loses its meaning and quantum uncertainty rules. At this level all known laws of physics break down and even space and time become nebulous concepts. Any and all conceivable distortions of spacetime will be <u>popping in and out of existence in a random and chaotic dance which is going on all the time everywhere in the universe.</u> Terms such as "quantum fluctuations" and the "quantum foam" which are used to describe this chaotic activity certainly do not do it justice."
-Jim Al-Khalili PhD, Black Holes, Wormholes, and Time Machines, pg. 207 PhD in Theoretical Nuclear Physics, theoretical physicist at the University of Surrey

The existence of these seemingly random particles does not violate the laws of physics, especially the Law of Conservation of Energy:

"Where did all these particles come from? The answer is that relativity and quantum mechanics allow matter to be created out of energy in the form of particle/antiparticle pairs. And where did the energy come from to create this matter? The answer is that it was borrowed from the gravitational energy of the universe. The universe has an enormous debt of negative gravitational energy, which exactly balances the positive energy of the matter."
-Stephen Hawking, PhD, Black Holes and Baby Universes, Pg. 97

Virtual particles have been shown, through experiments, to exist, as seen in the Lamb shift and the Casimir Effect.

"These particles are called virtual because, unlike "real" particles, they cannot be observed directly with a particle detector. Their indirect effects can nonetheless be measured, and **their existence has been confirmed** *by a small shift (the "Lamb shift") they produce in the spectrum of light from excited hydrogen atoms."*
-Stephen Hawking PhD, Black Holes and Baby Universes, Pg 107

Regarding the Casimir Effect,

"As we saw in Chapter 7, even what we think of as "empty" space is filled with pairs of virtual particles and antiparticles that appear together, move apart, and come back together and annihilate each other. Now, suppose one has two metal plates a short distance apart. The plates will act like mirrors for the virtual photons or particles of light. In fact they will form a cavity between them, a bit like an organ pipe that will resonate only at certain notes. This means that virtual photons can occur in the space between the plates only if their wavelengths (the distance between the crest of one wave and the next) fit a whole number of times into the gap between the plates. If the width of a cavity is a whole number of wavelengths plus a fraction of a wavelength, then after some reflections backward and forward between the plates, the crests of one wave with coincide with the troughs of another and the waves will cancel out. Because the virtual photons between the plates can have only the resonant wavelengths, there will be slightly fewer of them than in the region outside the plates where virtual photons can have any wavelength. Thus there will be slightly fewer virtual photons hitting the inside surfaces of the plates than the outside surfaces. One would therefore expect a force on the plates, pushing them toward each other. **This force has actually been detected and has the predicted value. Thus we have experimental evidence that virtual particles exist and have real effects.***"* -Stephen Hawking PhD, The Illustrated Brief History of Time, pgs. 204-206

Virtual particles can include all types of particles, including photons, electrons, gluons, bosons, and quarks. According to physicists, under certain conditions in the universe, virtual particles can exist for longer periods of time and therefore become "real" particles. This particular example relates to conditions of space near a black hole, but in principle this shows that science does generally allow for the possibility of virtual particles popping into existence and becoming real particles.

"We can understand this in the following way: what we think of as "empty" space cannot be completely empty because that would mean that all the fields, such as the gravitational and electromagnetic fields, would have to be exactly zero. However, the value of a field and its rate of change with time are like the position and velocity of a particle: the uncertainty

*principle implies that the more accurately one knows one of these quantities, the less accurately one can know the other. So in empty space the field cannot be fixed at exactly zero, because then it would have both a precise value (zero) and a precise rate of change (also zero). There must be a certain minimum amount of uncertainty, or quantum fluctuations, in the value of the field. One can think of these fluctuations as pairs of **particle of light or gravity** that appear together at some time, move apart, and then come together again and annihilate each other. These particles are virtual particles like carry the gravitational force of the sun: unlike real particles, they cannot be observed directly with a particle detector. However, their indirect effects, such as small changes in the electron orbits in atoms, can be measured and agree with the theoretical predictions to a remarkable degree of accuracy. The uncertainty principle also predicts that there will be similar **virtual pairs of matter particles, such as electrons or quarks**. In this case, however, one member of the pair will be a particle, and the other an antiparticle (the antiparticles of light and gravity are the same as the particles). Because energy cannot be created out of nothing, one of the partners in a particle/antiparticle pair will have positive energy, and the other partner negative energy. The one with negative energy is condemned to be a short-lived virtual particle because real particles always have positive energy in normal situations. It must therefore seek out its partner and annihilate with it. However, a real particle close to a massive body has less energy than if it were far away, because it would take energy to lift it far away against the gravitational attraction of the body. Normally, the energy of the particle is still positive, but the gravitational field inside a black hole is so strong that even a real particle can have negative energy there. It is therefore possible, if a black hole is present, for the **virtual particle** with negative energy to fall into the black hole and **become a real particle or antiparticle**. In this case it no longer has to annihilate with its partner. Its forsaken partner may fall into the black hole as well. Or, having positive energy, it might also escape from the vicinity of the black hole as **a real particle or antiparticle**. To an observer at a distance, it will appear to have been emitted from the black hole."*
-Stephen Hawking PhD, The Illustrated Brief History of Time, Pgs. 134-137

According to science it is possible that physical quantum particles can randomly pop into existence seemingly out of nowhere. If God is controlling the "quantum dice", then this means God could cause these subatomic quantum particles to come into existence out of nowhere. This does not contradict the laws of physics in any way. Rather the laws of physics and modern science make clear that subatomic quantum particles popping into existence from out of nowhere is the normal state of the universe, which science has confirmed. And it is entirely possible for this randomness to be controlled by God controlling the "quantum dice"; and the quantum randomness seen has no explanation. Metaphorically speaking, this is a huge hole in the wall of science, which allows for the hand of God to come through into the physical universe, without in any way contradicting science or the known laws of physics. This shows that science actually allows for miracles and the miraculous done by God, without it in any way conflicting with Science or Modern Physics.

Modern Physics teaches that elementary particles, of all kinds, can and do randomly pop in and out of existence. This includes photons, which are particles of light. This also includes gravitons, which are theoretical and theoretically instrumental in gravity, as well as gluons, bosons and other force carrying particles.

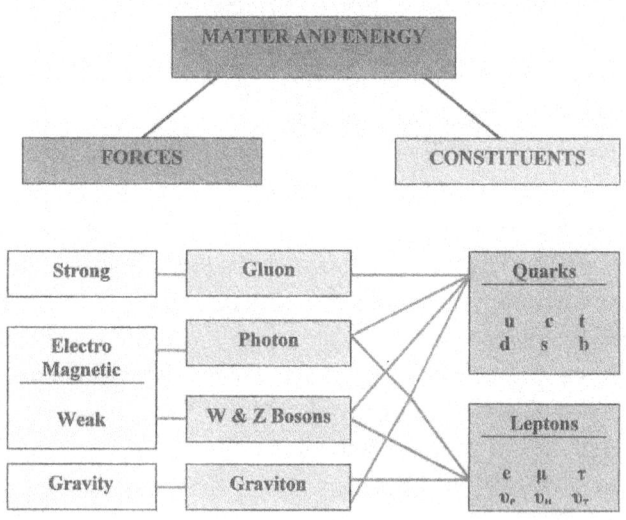

Some force carrying particles are what hold quarks together to form neutrons and protons, and other force particles hold together atoms. All of these particles can pop into existence out of nowhere, seemingly randomly, the universe allows for this, and the universe was created by God intentionally to be the way it is.

What are quarks and electrons? They are the particles that are the building blocks of atoms.

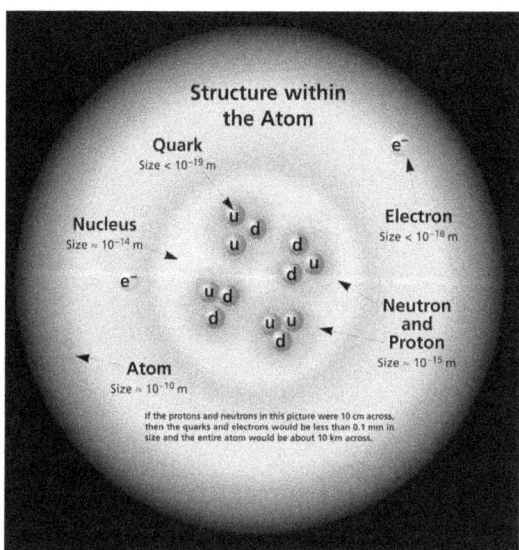

Different types of atoms make up all of the elements of matter, as seen in the periodic table of the elements.

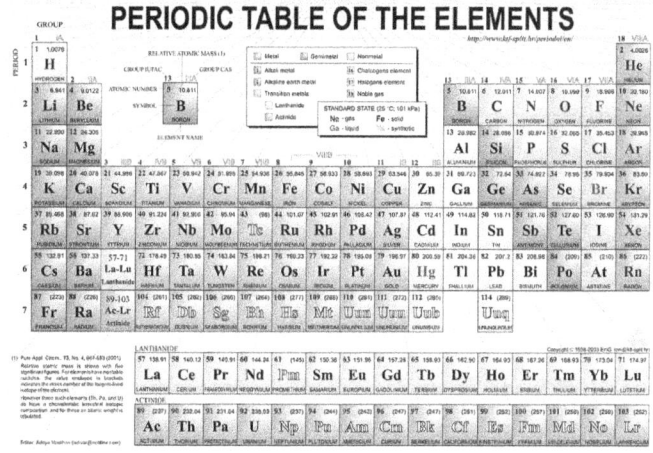

Atoms are the building blocks of all the matter we see, and our bodies are made of atoms.

So assuming God, who is omnipotent, one way or another controlled the randomness of the quantum world... then this means that God could choose to have a large number of quarks, gluons, electrons, etc. pop into existence very quickly, and assemble into atoms. God could also do this in such a way that many atoms were formed, and would assemble into much larger objects, even objects large enough that we could see them.

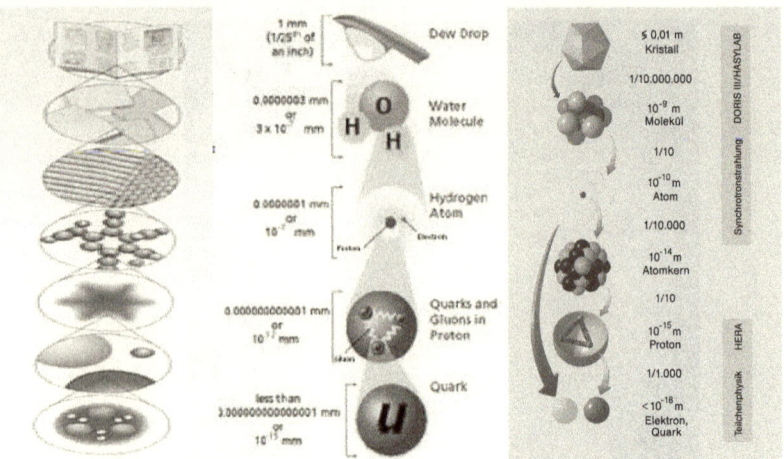

This might include things like oil and grain popping into existence out of nowhere:

1 Kings 17:8-16
And the word of the LORD came unto him, saying, Arise, get thee to Zarephath, which belongeth to Zidon, and dwell there: behold, I have commanded a widow woman there to sustain thee. So he arose and went to Zarephath. And when he came to the gate of the city, behold, the widow woman was there gathering of sticks: and he called to her, and said, Fetch me, I pray thee, a little water in a vessel, that I may drink. And as she was going to fetch it, he called to her, and said, Bring me, I pray thee, a morsel of bread in thine hand. And she said, As the LORD thy God liveth, I have not a cake, but an handful of meal in a barrel, and a little oil in a cruse: and, behold, I am gathering two sticks, that I may go in and dress it for me and my son, that we may eat it, and die. And Elijah said unto her, Fear not; go and do as thou hast said: but make me thereof a little cake first, and bring it unto me, and after make for thee and for thy son. For thus saith the LORD God of Israel, The

<u>barrel of meal shall not waste, neither shall the cruse of oil fail, until the day that the LORD sendeth rain upon the earth.</u> And she went and did according to the saying of Elijah: and she, and he, and her house, did eat many days. <u>And the barrel of meal wasted not, neither did the cruse of oil fail, according to the word of the LORD, which he spake by Elijah.</u>

God provided for 3 years oil and grain, though the land was in a drought with famine. This oil and grain appeared seemingly out of thin air. But another way to put it might be that it appeared out of "seemingly random quantum foam". And there are many miracles, signs, and wonders in the Bible, done by God, which are similar to this, such as Jesus Christ feeding the multitudes of thousands from a couple fish and a few loaves of bread.

Also, there are miraculous healings mentioned many times in the Bible. According to science, our bodies are made up of molecules of atoms, which are made from quarks and electrons and such. Consider the cases of sight being restored to the blind, the healing of the disfigured hand, the healing of lepers, and the healing of all manner of sicknesses; miracles done by Jesus Christ. Control over the "quantum dice" would be one way to explain how sick flesh was instantaneously changed into healthy flesh.

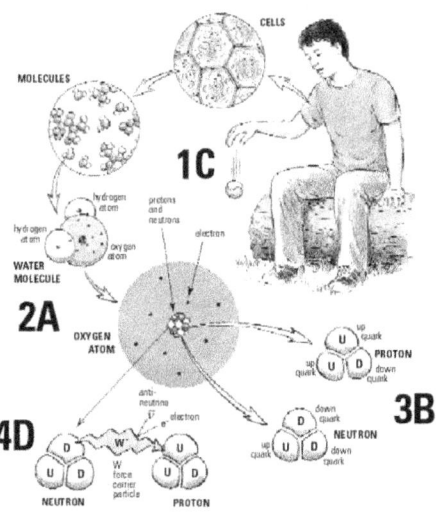

And so this is one way to describe, in modern physics concepts, how God does miracles, signs, and wonders. Though God does do them, whether control of the "quantum dice" of quantum physics is truly and specifically how, or not.

But the Bible also says that Holy angels, and Fallen angels, also work miracles, signs and wonders. (Acts 2:22, 5:12, 2 Peter 2:11, Heb 2:4, Matt 24:24, 2 Thes 2:9, Rev 13:2, 14, 16:14) So it could be an accurate description to say that how fallen angels also do miracles, signs, and wonders is because they too somehow have control over the "quantum dice", though definitely on a more limited scale than God does. The Bible teaches that God is everywhere in the universe, and there is nowhere that He is not. Whereas fallen angels have a set, limited, location for their spirit body, and are only in one place at a time, much like mankind. Under this line of reasoning, God has power, and "quantum power" over everywhere in the universe, but fallen angels only have power or "quantum power" in their immediate location. Also, God has power over the fallen angels' spirit bodies themselves, as their bodies are part of the creation, whereas fallen angels have no such power over God.

It does make some analogous sense that all angels would have powers like God, but limited, for the Bible several times in the Old Testament calls angels the "sons of God". (Gen 6, Job 1:6, Job 2:1, Psalm 29:1, 89:6)

It may be that the extra-dimensionality of angels is what would make possible them having limited control over the "quantum dice" in their immediate location.

"Today, however, physicists are following a different trail-the one leading to superstring theory. Unlike previous proposals, it has survived every blistering mathematical challenge ever hurled at it. Not surprisingly, the theory is a radical-some might say crazy-departure from the past, being based on tiny strings vibrating in 10-dimensional space-time... In superstring theory, the subatomic particles we see in nature are nothing more than different resonances of the vibrating superstrings, in the same way that different musical notes emanate from the different modes of vibration of a violin string."

-Michio Kaku PhD, "Into the Eleventh Dimension", author of Hyperspace: A Scientific Odyssey through the 10th Dimension, Oxford University Press.

According to String Theory, particles in the 4-dimenional space-time we observe, are the result of vibrations of 1 dimensional strings that exist in an additional 6-7 dimensions, in the scientific sense of the word (which comes to 10-11 dimensions total).

As such, speaking generally according to science in principle, it is possible that the extra-dimensionality of angels would allow for their altering of particles in our 4 dimensional world, on the subatomic quantum level. As such, their extra-dimensionality, in the spiritual realm, may be tied directly to their ability to work "miracles, signs, and wonders", possibly through being able to determine how the "quantum dice" fall (on a limited scale in their immediate locality).

To illustrate, imagine that sitting on a table, is a cup. This cup has 3 spatial dimensions, and as the second pass, it moves through the 4th dimension of time. Now, in the exact same location as the cup, would be 6-7 invisible dimensions that you can't see. And that is because these invisible 6-7 dimensions intersect the 4 dimensions we know at every point. These 6-7 dimensions are most definitely not somewhere else, but are in the same place we are, but invisible. Now, if these 6-7 extra dimensions correspond to the invisible spiritual realm that the Bible teaches, then an angel who has a spirit body would have an invisible spirit body comprised of the stuff of these 6-7 extra dimensions. And such an invisible angel could choose to effect the 6-7 extra dimensions where the cup is located so as to knock the cup over.

In other words, fallen angels have spirit bodies in the invisible spiritual realm. If the spiritual realm is composed of these extra 6-7 dimensions, then the spirit bodies of the fallen angels are composed of the spiritual realm, these extra 6-7 dimensions. Just as the invisible spiritual realm is all around us, so also could be these 6-7 extra dimensions. According to String Theory (just a theory) what we observe as an effect in our 3 spatial dimensions is caused by what happens in the 6-7 invisible extra dimensions. This means that an extra-dimensional angel could use their extra-dimensional spirit body in the 6-7 extra dimensions, to have the effect of changing things in the physical 3 dimensions we perceive. And in this, fallen angels would also have limited control over how the "quantum dice" fall, but only in a very limited location where they are present. As the invisible realm is all around us (or these extra dimensions would be also) a fallen angel can only effect changes in the immediate locality around them, in the location of their spirit body.

And so this shows how Modern Physics also allows for angels or fallen angels to work miracles (in a limited locality) along the same lines as how Modern Physics allows for God to work miracles. And so angels can also work miracles and do the miraculous, without violating and laws of Modern Physics or science. Rather, Modern Physics and Science totally allows for the existence of angels, their spirit bodies, the invisible spiritual realm, and the miraculous powers of angels as described in the Bible.

When it comes to Holy angels or fallen angels, the Bible describes that they can cause dreams and Visions, as well as causing the physically miraculous or miracles.

In the case of fallen angels, they cause False Visions, which can seem entirely physically real to a victim, and also dreams. Beyond this fallen angels can cause physical injury, and other sorts of physical manifestations, like objects moving, or recording film being altered, etc. These physical manifestations would be considered as false signs, false miracles, and false wonders, Biblically speaking.

I think that fallen angels being able to control (in their immediate locality) how the "quantum dice" fall, would work as a way to explain Physical manifestations very easily, both with visible angels materializing, or seeing the physical effects of invisible angels, including the physical aspects of Visions.

Excepting time perception manipulation, I also think this "quantum dice" idea explains all varieties and aspects of Visions quite well, and also dreams. This is because the human brain also can experience the effects of a fallen angel being able to control the "quantum dice" (in a limited localized way).

"The human brain, however, is also subject to the uncertainty principle. Thus, there is an element of the randomness associated with quantum mechanics in human behavior. But the energies involved in the brain are low, so quantum mechanical uncertainty is only a small effect."
-Stephen Hawking PhD, Black Holes and Baby Universes, Pg. 133

Although the effect of quantum mechanical uncertainty in the brain is normally small, if fallen angels can determine how the "quantum dice" fall, then a fallen angel could make the effect quite large and noticeable.

Regarding False Visions, all of our physical senses are dependant on how our brain interprets them. By fallen angels generating electrical impulses in the brain, and such things like that, fallen angels would be able to make us "see" things that are not actually in front of our eyes, and "hear" things that are not there to make any sound, "feel" things that are not touching our bodies, "smell" things not before our noses, and "taste" things that are not on our tongues. These things would seem completely real to all of the bodily senses. And the electrical impulses that are truly transmitting information about reality around us could also be blocked out by fallen angels, under this same ability. Or actual reality could be partially blocked. And either way, false electrical signals in the brain generated by fallen angels, through manipulation of the "quantum dice", could cause a person to experience a False Vision that seemed entirely physically real, but was not.

A person could be caused to perceive something completely illusionary, by a fallen angel manipulating that person's brain, which is a person's gateway to physical perception. As such, an illusion could seem completely physically real to all of the bodily senses, so much so as to be completely indistinguishable from reality to the person. This manipulation of the senses through manipulation of the brain is very likely what happens in False Vision (or in Holy angelic true Visions). Fallen angels could cause this to happen to more than one person at a time, strengthening the deception. And also under the same limited control over the "quantum dice", fallen angels could cause physical manifestations, even running concurrently with a Vision which seems real. This sort of deception can be very powerful. Dreams could be explained much in the same way, but the same sort of thing occurring while the person is asleep and dreaming.

Besides all of this, there is one more thing which is miraculous that fallen angels do, which modern science allows for in a specific way. That is time perception manipulation.

Chapter 9: Modern Physics and the Abilities of Fallen Angels
Time Perception Manipulation

Luke 4:5 "And **the devil, taking him up** into an high mountain, shewed unto him all the kingdoms of the world in a moment of time."

This case of Satan likely causing Jesus Christ to have a Vision, as mentioned in the Bible, was likely at least hours in less than 1 second.

Let's look at some of the examples of time perception manipulation mentioned earlier:

The case of Robert was about 2 hours in about 1 minute.
The Valdes case was about 5 days in 15 minutes.
The case of Michael was about 20 years in about 7 days.

In a seconds-to-second ratio, this equates to:

Robert: 7200 seconds in 60 seconds,
or a ratio of <u>120 seconds in 1 second</u>

Valdes: 432,000 seconds in 900 seconds,
ratio of <u>480 seconds in 1 second</u>

Michael: 630,720,000 seconds in 604,800 seconds,
ratio <u>1043 seconds in 1 second</u>

What we are going to cover next is the time perception manipulation abilities of fallen angels, as seen in False Visions. I will first be covering the ways time perception manipulation can **not** be explained under Modern Science, before I get into the way it can be explained, and Modern Physics allows for this.

First off, it is necessary to keep in mind that the memories of these experiences are of real interaction between the abductee, and the vision caused by the fallen angel, in which the abductee can make choices while the experience is ongoing.

I would first like to make the point that remembered False Vision experiences are not memories that are ready-made and downloaded like a file into the abductee's brain. Rather, because the abductee actively participates in decision making during the Vision, the experience is stored as the events take place, over time. In short, what abductees usually experience is very different than what some people refer to as "false memories". This can be sufficiently supported in that there are cases in which an abductee has experienced a couple hours worth of abduction, called out to Jesus for help, the experience has abruptly stopped, and the abductee has found that only minutes had passed since the experience had begun, not hours. As Satan does not work against Satan, a fallen angel would not download a ready-made memory story that included the abduction experience stopping in the name and authority of Jesus Christ.

So this shows that abductees are able to make decisions during the False Vision experience. It is a real experience, that takes place over the gradual progression of the experience, and it progresses with time passing. It is reported that the flow of time seems normal to abductees during these experiences, along with the experience feeling real to all the bodily senses.

As the brain of the victim of a False Vision is an integral part of how fallen angels carry out these Visions, and the memories of these attacks are stored in the brain, then the time perception manipulation aspect of these attacks must be explainable in a way that is consistent and not conflicting with the physical human brain and how it functions. And so any explanation of time perception manipulation must be limited and confined to explanations that do not conflict with the science of the human brain.

In examining this further, I am going to keep relevant and prevalent in this explanation that it has been shown in False Visions that time perception manipulation is present while the abductee's body does not go anywhere. This is important. I would assert that any solution that would work to explain time perception manipulation in this scenario would also work in all other scenarios, though the opposite would not be true. The simplest answer can be found in explaining the most restrictive scenario in difficulty of a science-friendly explanation.

If we were to assume that time perception manipulation involves a compacting or compressing of extensive experiences into a short period of time, then this would require the human brain to handle in one second, somewhere from a hundred to a thousand times more information than the brain usually processes in one second. The brain processes information by the firing of neurons.

The only information I could find on neurons firing more rapidly than normal were studies on psychoactive drugs, heroin especially. As people attacked by fallen angels that experience time perception manipulation do not report experiencing a severe heroin-like sensation, this serves as experimental evidence that overly-rapid neuronic firing in the normal passage of time will not work to explain this time perception manipulation.

And as such, time perception manipulation does not involve a compacting or compressing of extensive experiences into a short period of time. The only other option is that these experiences actually do take as much time as subjectively perceived by the person having a fallen angelic Vision, though objective time passage for the rest of the world is much shorter.

A major example for this may be seen in the theory of general relativity. According to relativity, no matter what speed a person moves, time is perceived to pass at the same rate. However, less time will comparatively pass for an accelerated person than for a (relatively) stationary person. Yet either person will feel time passing at the same rate. It could be argued from a theological standpoint that God designed the human brain to need a consistent flow of actual time in order to function correctly, and designed a universe in which time passage would remain consistent, no matter to what speed a human might accelerate.

Because the person's brain is involved in the process of a Vision, yet their body does not go anywhere, many theoretical physics concepts dealing with time would not work to explain how the brain can experience more time while the body experiences less time.

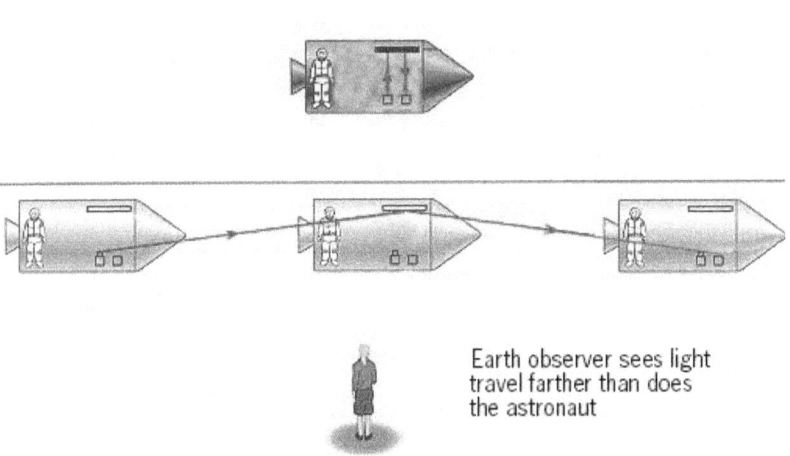

Earth observer sees light travel farther than does the astronaut

Could general relativity and time dilation explain how this works? Relativistic Time Dilation would not work, because it would require the body to feel acceleration (or its gravitational equivalent) in comparison to the brain, at over 99% the speed of light. This speed would be necessary to produce a 100 or 1000 seconds to 1 second ratio. This is not what is reported by witnesses of the person under attack's body, that see it does not go anywhere, nor the Biblical account that during Visions people do not go anywhere. So this cannot be the case, aside from the fact that such a thing would likely kill the person.

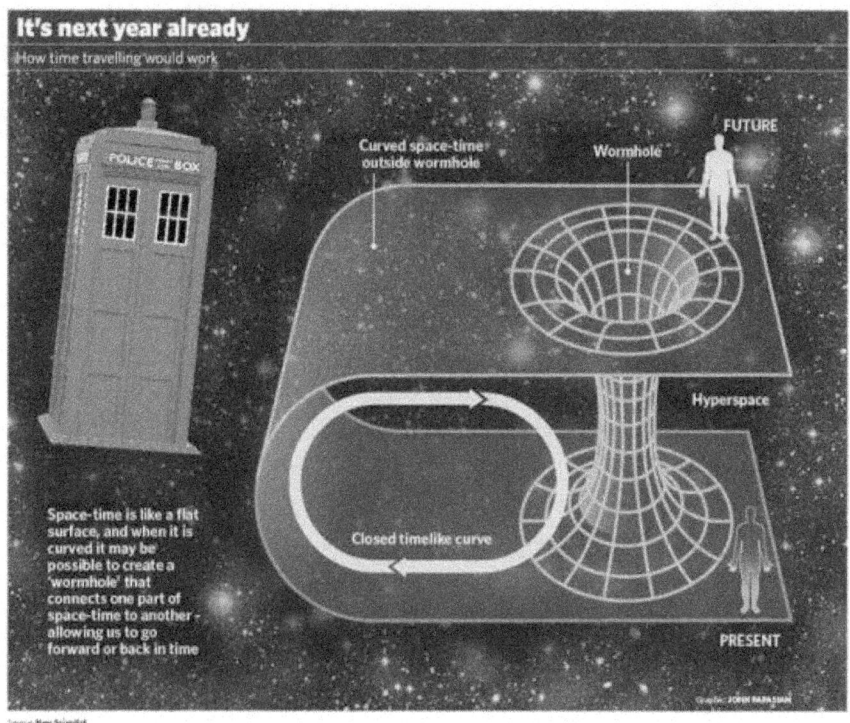

Could time travel gained by travel to the future, and then the past, explain this extra perceived time?

There is a type of theoretical wormhole, called a CTC, which was once theorized to be able to be used in this way, if many detailed criteria were met. But according to the current consensus of scientists, a CTC would not work for time travel to the future or past. This manner specifically would involve moving a brain to another location in 4d space-time, spending a real amount of time in that other location moving into the future, and then the brain traveling back in time to the same moment it left. Even if this could work without killing the person, a CTC wormhole still would not work for returning the brain to the past, as a CTC will not work for time travel to the past or future. A CTC wormhole will not work for time travel to the future and past for a brain, or a person, or even for a bowling ball, as they cannot be used for time travel in general.

Kip Thorne and Stephen Hawking had an ongoing debate for about 20 years over the subject of time travel into the past, using a CTC wormhole for time travel. The debate, based on their books, seems to have become settled, with Thorne (pro-possibility of time travel) coming to agree with Hawking (anti-possibility of time travel). Here are some highlights:

"*Perhaps fortunately for our survival (and that of our mothers), it seems that the laws of physics do not allow such time travel. There seems to be a Chronology Protection Agency that makes the world safe for historians by preventing travel into the past. What seems to happen is that the effects of the uncertainty principle would cause there to be a large amount of radiation if one traveled into the past. This radiation would either warp space-time so much that it would not be possible to go back in time, or it would cause space-time to come to an end in a singularity like the big bang and the big crunch. Either way, our past would be safe from evil-minded persons. The Chronology Protection Hypothesis is supported by some recent calculations that I and other people have done. But the best evidence we have that time travel is not possible, and never will be, is that we have not been invaded by hordes of tourists from the future.*"
-Stephen Hawking PhD, Black Holes and Baby Universes Pg. 154 (1994)

"*Translating back the viewpoint of an observer at rest in the wormhole (the observer that Kim and I had relied on), Hawking's conjecture meant that the quantum gravity cutoff occurs 10^{-95} second before the wormhole becomes a time machine, not 10^{-43} second – and by then, according to our calculations, the vacuum fluctuational beam is strong enough, but just barely so, that it might indeed destroy the wormhole.*"
-Kip S. Thorne PhD, Black Holes and Time Warps pg. 520 (1994)

"*Hawking suspects that the growing beams of vacuum fluctuations is nature's way of enforcing chronology protection: Whenever one tries to make a time machine, and no matter what kind of device one uses in one's attempt (a wormhole, a spinning cylinder, a "cosmic string", or whatever), just before one's device becomes a time machine, a beam of vacuum fluctuations will circulate through the device and destroy it. Hawking seems ready to bet heavily on this outcome. I am not willing to take the other side in such a bet. I do enjoy taking bets with Hawking, but only bets that I have a reasonable chance of winning. My strong gut*

feeling is that I would lose this one. My own calculations with Kim, and unpublished calculations that Eanna Flanagan (a student of mine) has done more recently, suggest to me that Hawking is likely to be right. Every time machine is likely to self-destruct (by means of circulating vacuum fluctuations) at the moment one tries to activate it."
-Kip S. Thorne PhD, Black Holes and Time Warps pg. 521 (1994)

That was all from 1994, but a more recent quote from 2001 shows the issue has generally been settled:

"... Since the sum-over-histories calculations in these backgrounds are mathematically equivalent, one can conclude that the probability of these backgrounds goes to zero as they approach the warping needed for time loops. In other words, the probability of having sufficient warping for a time machine is zero. This supports what I have called the **Chronology Protection Conjecture:** *that the laws of physics conspire to prevent time travel by macroscopic objects.*
Although time loops are allowed by the sum over histories, the probabilities are extremely small. Based on the duality arguments I mentioned earlier, I estimate the probability that Kip Thorne could go back and kill his grandfather as less than one in ten with a trillion trillion trillion trillion trillion zeroes after it... As gambling men, **Kip and I would bet on odds like that. The trouble is, we can't bet each other because we are now both on the same side."**
-Stephen Hawking PhD, The Universe in a Nutshell, pgs. 152-153 (2001)

One problem with time travel to the past (and future) between 2 locations in 4d space-time, is that, put simply, electromagnetic vacuum fluctuations would build up traveling in a loop from the present to the past, an infinite loop, and this would destroy any pathway from the present to the past (or future). Stephen Hawking and Kip Thorne have said, CTC wormholes won't work for time travel.

As such, this is also not a possibility for time perception manipulation during a fallen angel attack, and it can summarily be concluded that peoples' brains do not go anywhere, or time travel. Time gained by traveling to the future, and then the past, is not allowed by physics in any way that would fit this time perception manipulation scenario seen in a fallen angelic Vision.

Biblically, this can be understood in that God created the universe so as to not allow time travel into the past. God controls both sides of the wormhole, and it is God who would make it so electromagnetic vacuum fluctuations in a loop from the wormhole mouths would destroy the wormhole before it could allow for any possible time travel.

God created time, as did Jesus Christ, as all things were created through Him.

Jesus Christ says:
Rev 22:13 I am the Alpha and the Omega, the First and the Last, the Beginning and the End.

As such God has complete authority over time, and simply does not allow time travel to the past, or the future and then the past again.

None of these theories mentioned will work as an explanation for time perception manipulation caused by fallen angels during False Visions. So then what is going on?

The key verse is Luke 4:5
"And the devil, taking him up into an high mountain, shewed unto him all the kingdoms of the world in a moment of time."

This verse does not describe time travel to the past. In contrast, this verse describes a long period of time passing during a second, or less than a second. Or another way to say this is that some extra time was perceptually gained by the person, more than the objective passage of time that God controls. This verse describes a long period of time passing during a second, or less than a second. Or another way to say this is that some extra time was perceptually gained by the person, more than the objective passage of time that God controls.

So how would a fallen angel do this? How might this work?

The answer is that there is simply more to the dimension of time than we normally think of there being. I believe the Bible sets precedence for this concept, and this is how I would interpret Joshua's Long Day.

Josh 10:12-14
Then spake Joshua to the LORD in the day when the LORD delivered up the Amorites before the children of Israel, and he said in the sight of Israel, Sun, stand thou still upon Gibeon; and thou, Moon, in the valley of Ajalon. And the sun stood still, and the moon stayed, until the people had avenged themselves upon their enemies. Is not this written in the book of Jasher? So the sun stood still in the midst of heaven, and hasted not to go down about a whole day. And there was no day like that before it or after it, that the LORD hearkened unto the voice of a man: for the LORD fought for Israel.

I have read several theories to explain how this worked, but here is mine:

When God made the dimension of time, He made it to have both its flow in length, as we normally perceive, and draw as a line, but also to have a width to it, at right angles to its length. This width is normally small and tight like a string. But the width of time is like a stretchy material, like a rubber band, and so if God wants to, God can stretch out the width of time. The width of time is not affected by the 3 dimensions of space, or things like gravity or speed. The length of time is what is referred to in "space-time", but the width of time exists unaffected by the things that would normally affect the length of time. In other words, the width of time works like a 2nd dimension to time.

In Joshua's Long Day, it was the width of time that God stretched out, around the surface of the earth, and for the people on the earth. As such the people on earth experienced long time passage in the width of time, during what was a brief moment in the length of time.

I believe that according to physics this is possible. Although the concept of time having a 2nd dimension of "width" seems to be in its infancy, there is some information to be found on it. The concept which parallels the "width" of time in modern theoretical physics is the concept of "imaginary time":

"...One of these is that it is easier to do the sum if one deals with histories in what is called imaginary time rather than in ordinary, real time. Imaginary time is a difficult concept to grasp, and it is probably the one that has caused the greatest problems for the readers of my book. I have also been criticized fiercely by philosophers for using imaginary time. **How can imaginary time have anything to do with the real universe?**
I think these philosophers have not learned the lessons of history. It was once considered obvious that the earth was flat and that the sun went around the earth, yet since the time of Copernicus and Galileo, we have had to adjust to the idea that the earth is round and that it goes around the sun. Similarly, it was long obvious that time went for the same rate for every observer, but since Einstein, we have had to accept that time goes for at different rates for different observers. It also seemed obvious that the universe had a unique history, yet since the discovery of quantum mechanics, we have had to consider the universe as having every possible history. **I want to suggest that the idea of imaginary time is something that we will also have to come to accept. It is an intellectual leap of the same order as believing that the world is round. I think that imaginary time will come to seem as natural as a round earth does now.** *There are not many Flat Earthers left in the educated world."*
-Stephen Hawking, Black Holes and Baby Universe, Pg. 81-82

Imaginary time *is already a commonplace of science fiction. But **it is more than science fiction or a mathematical trick. It is something that shapes the universe we live in.***
-Stephen Hawking, Black Holes and Baby Universes, Pg. 83

Though it is a newer concept, it seems that imaginary time shapes the universe we live in. According to physics, what is it like?

"You can think of ordinary, real time as a horizontal line, going from left to right. Early times are on the left, and late times are on the right. But you can also consider another direction of time, up and down the page. This is the so-called imaginary direction of time, at right angles to real time.
What is the point of introducing the concept of imaginary time? Why doesn't one just stick to the ordinary, real time that we understand? The reason is that, as noted earlier, matter and energy tend to make space-time curve in on itself. In the real time direction, this inevitably leads to singularities, places where space-time comes to an end. At the singularities, the equations of physics cannot be defined; thus one cannot predict what will happen. **But the imaginary time direction is at right angles to real time.** *This means that it behaves in a similar way to the three directions that correspond to moving in space. The curvature of space-time caused by the matter in the universe can then lead to the three space directions and the imaginary time direction meeting up around the back. They would form a closed surface, like the surface of the earth.* **The space directions and imaginary time would form a space-time that was closed in on itself, without boundaries or edges. It wouldn't have any point that could be called a beginning or end, any more than the surface of the earth has a beginning or end."**
-Stephen Hawking PhD, Black Holes and Baby Universes, Pg 82

"When one tried to unify gravity with quantum mechanics, one had to introduce the idea of "imaginary" time. Imaginary time is indistinguishable from directions in space. If one can go north, one can turn around and head south; equally, if one can go forward in imaginary time, one out to be able to turn round and go backward. **This means that there can be no important difference between the forward and backward directions of imaginary time.** *On the other hand, when one looks at "real" time, there's a very big difference between the forward and backward directions, as we all know."*
-Stephen Hawking PhD, The Illustrated Brief History of Time, Pg 182

Imaginary time does not follow the forward direction of time, but instead forms a closed loop, in which there is no distinguishable forward or backward direction. This concept seems to parallel a stretchy width to time very well. A person experiencing imaginary time could gain time, going around a closed loop on the width of time, and ending up where they started. This would allow time to be gained, and experienced, by the person, without that person moving forward on the length of time, save a moment.

Could the science theory of Imaginary Time, or concept of a Width to Time, explain time perception manipulation in False Visions caused by fallen angels? …**Yes.**

As I have mentioned before, the Bible calls the angels the "sons of God" in several places, and this may relate to that angels can do many of the same things that God can do, but on a more limited and local basis.

For instance, God can perform miracles, signs and wonders, and Joshua's Long Day was one of these miraculous events. If this analogy holds true in this case, as it has in other cases, then it would make sense that fallen angels may also be able to stretch out the width of time on a limited local basis. The length of time God keeps all authority over, and fallen angels cannot travel it nor stretch it out. But during a Vision the additional time perceived would be from fallen angels stretching out the width of time (not the length of time). Time is received like a substance coming from the width of time, while there is scarcely anything gained in the ever-proceeding length of time.

In fallen angelic Vision experiences, this could be visualized as a fallen angel stretching out the width of time around the brain of the person under attack. The person's brain does Not leave their body, nor move forwards and backwards along the length of time. But the person does experience a gain of time from the period in which the width of time is stretched out around their brain. This allows for a gain of perceived passage of time in a Vision, and would allow for a couple minutes to or even a couple hours to be perceived to pass in a moment, or second.

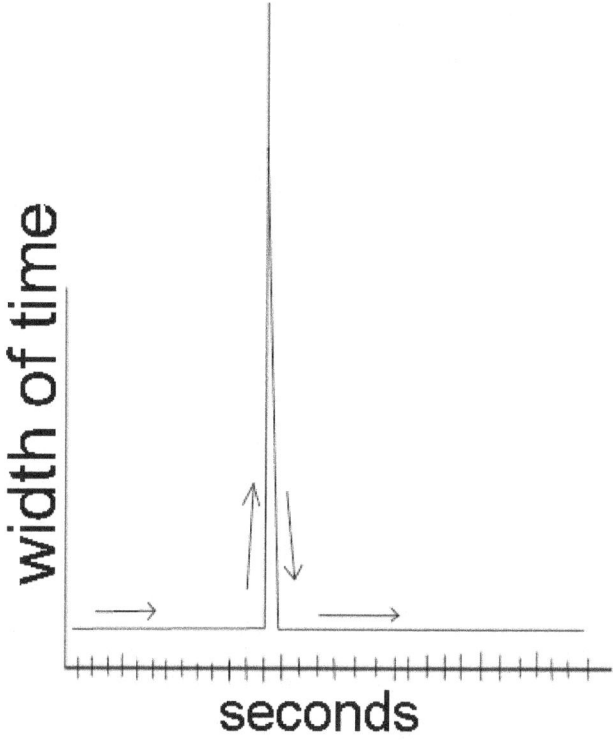

A **length of time** Ω

minutes/hours in a second

This scenario would allow the brain to function at its normal speed, with decision making processes working as they normally do in the brain-mind-soul-spirit connection. This would also allow for memories to be stored in the brain according to the normal way the brain functions.

And so this is how I would explain fallen angels accomplish time perception manipulation during Visions. Modern Physics seems to somewhat allow for this, especially that angels might be able to do this under the explanation of if they were extra-dimensional in 6-7 extra dimensions, they might be able to access a second dimension of time as well. In any case, this explanation of stretching the width of time around the brain of the person would work to explain time perception manipulation in Visions.

Chapter 10 - Conclusions

I find a good analogy to conceptualize an extra dimension or dimensions is the green code in the Matrix movie. Like the agents in the Matrix movie, fallen angels can alter the "code" ("quantum dice") to change what is there and alter the green code inside a person's mind, to change what the person perceives, through their brain.

As such I often try to represent the abilities of Fallen angels and the False Visions they cause, using Matrix imagery. I use a red sphere of code to represent the invisible extra-dimensional or spiritual realm fallen angel. (hallway is green, sphere is red)

As an example, below is a close up of a fallen angel False Vision of an "alien abduction". Remember that the entire vision, all 3 aliens, and the setting, are all caused by 1 fallen angel. In this example, the red ball below contains a person standing in a room with 3 aliens, near a table, in a defensive posture against the aliens. That is how the person having this Vision experiences themself to be, and it seems real to them, though a Vision.

What this represents is that because of a fallen angel, the neurons in the person's brain are firing in such as way that their perceptions have been altered. As the person perceives their surroundings through their brain, which is the hub and gateway to all the physical senses, the true green reality has been blocked out either fully or partially, and the person perceives what is going on in the red sphere, which is the fallen angel attacking. Their brain being able to send signals of sensing the green reality around them has been blocked, and instead the deceptive red signals of the fallen angel is what is getting through to their brain. In the most extreme case, this can mean the person may perceive being touched, when they are not, smell things, see things, etc. which seem entirely physically real, but are not. These physical sensations can be of things which are external to the body, like the skin being cut, or internal to the body, such as John's stomach ache in Revelation, or any other sort of internal pain.

Because of the brain-sensory-hacking abilities of fallen angels seen in False Visions, which can seem completely physically real, it can be difficult to be able to tell with certainty that an actual pure physical manifestation of a fallen angel has occurred. Perhaps one example is that of fallen angels manifesting as UFOs (or whatever) in which pictures or video-recording have been taken.

It has to be kept in mind that when fallen angels do physically manifest, it may only be on a very limited and partial basis. One example is the audio-recordings made of ghosts, which if not hoaxes, only show a physical manifestation of the air vibrating so as to produce a recordable sound, or a physical manifestation to alter the recording device directly. That is all that could be proven to have occurred, at most. In fact in many cases, it is possible that a physical manifestation was limited to only a direct altering of the film or recording device, whether pictures of ghosts or UFOs, video film, or audio recordings, while people sometimes experience a False Vision in conjunction with this.

It is analogously similar to the scene in the movie The Matrix where Neo lays down on a table, and his brain is connected to a piece of hardware. He awakes to find himself standing in a white room, with Morpheus, and some chairs. He touches them and asks "Is this real?" and Morpheus comments to him on how what seems to be real is determined by electrical signals in the brain.
All of Neo's senses were working, it seemed real to him, yet it was not, and he wasn't really where he perceived himself to be: he was still on the table, where his brain and senses had been hacked into, blocking out reality, and replacing it with something that felt just as real, but was not. But, he really did have the experience.

This represents what the person perceives during the False Vision:

In this example, the person does not perceive the green reality, but only the red deception of the fallen angel. They may have a dream of being in this room with 3 aliens, or the Vision could seem to completely physically-real-seeming to the abductee, clear and focused as if they were fully awake. To an observer, the abductee might seem to be awake as normal, or in a trance/sleeping state, and the observer who is not under attack does not experience what the abductee is experiencing. It is possible for and observer to also get attacked, and perceive themselves to be in the room with the abductee, but then the observer would be represented with the same representation as the abductee above. It is also possible that the abductee could be allowed to perceive the green reality to some extent or another, making the mental attack only partial, and not full, such as a sensation of their actual body (in green reality) getting tapped by an observer. Or as in some cases, the abductee might see a gray, which seems physically real, overlaid on top of the green reality of their actual home, bedroom, car, etc. This would perhaps be better represented by a partially transparent red circle, in which some green is seen through the red.

Also lumped into the aspects of False Visions are events involving time perception manipulation. As in the case of Robert, the explanation is that in the localized area of his brain, something like a second dimension of time, ever present but at right-angles to the normal flow of time, was utilized by the fallen angel, so that he experienced hours in minutes. Again, we know this is possible for fallen angels to utilize time this way to a limited localized extent, on a person, as the Bible records in Luke 4:5 in Satan showing Jesus all the kingdoms of the world in the time it takes to blink. (And that God did this to a worldwide extent as in Joshua 10 as the sun stood still in the sky all day, though it should be noted nothing in the Bible indicates that fallen angels can do this in a worldwide way, nor beyond the localized effect on a person during a False Vision.)

As to Physical Manifestation, the major example I have used here is of the Malmstrom incident, in which UFOs were seen, and physical documented malfunctions, without any other explanation to be had, coincided with the UFOs.

In the case of abductees, partial physical manifestations are documented with bruises and other injuries, etc., however typically the simpler explanation for much of the experience is that the rest of the experience was a False Vision. Most of the experience was a False Vision, which also had minor elements of physical manifestation. For instance, an abductee flown around Mars and back in a UFO, who returns with a bruise, should be assumed to have had a False Vision of going to Mars. This is because a bruise that is ascertained to have been received during the experience is only able to serve as evidence of a partial limited physical manifestation of a fallen angel, only enough to produce a bruise. Along the same lines, cuts or scars, whether external or internal (such as to the sexual organs) would need to be ascertained to have been received during the experience, and could only serve as evidence of a partial limited physical manifestation of a fallen angel, only enough to produce those cuts or scars. A bruise as the only evidence simply cannot prove someone physically went to Mars.

When it come to physical manifestation, it is clear from the Bible that fallen angels can cause illness, as is seen in the case of Job being given boils by Satan, and Herod (accepting worship as a "god") being smitten with worms by an angel of God, which killed him. In this case of illness, once a fallen angel has caused an illness, it can remain for some time. One such illness that seems to be reported often among female abductees is that of "false pregnancy", which is a verifiable medical condition. This medical condition also happens to many women who have never reported having any "alien abduction" experiences. The symptoms include extended abdomen, sensations of a baby moving inside, menstrual changes and lack of menses, verifiable hormonal changes, weight gain, tender breasts, morning sickness, cervical changes, and false labor. Research has shown 18% of cases of false pregnancy were at one time diagnosed as a pregnancy by a doctor. This is likely as doctors use hormone blood tests. In the normal population this is estimated to occur 1-6 times per every 22,000 births. False pregnancy happens to many women who are not abductees. As such it is possible either that a fallen angel could supernaturally trigger this illness in a woman's body by a partial physical manifestation targeted to cause this illness, or could simply be playing upon an illness of false pregnancy that would have occurred in that women anyway, due to some natural or unrelated reason for this medical problem. To date there is no verifiable proof of any real "alien" conception taking place, or resulting babies, to be found in abduction research. (<u>From Wikipedia, False Pregnancy</u>).

Here is a False Vision combined with some degree of Physical Manifestation:

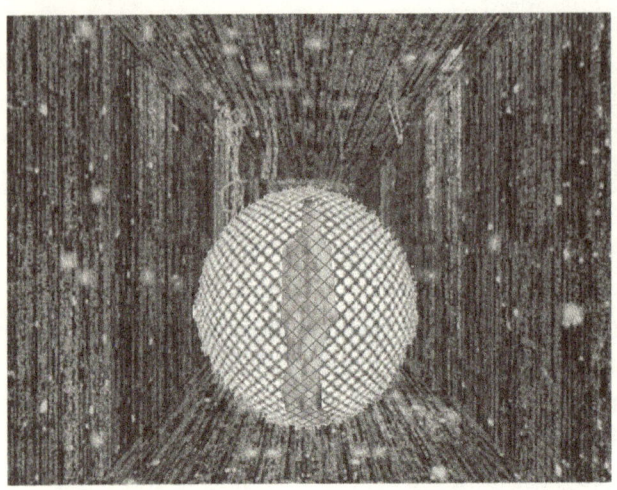

And what the person perceives during the combination False Vision / physical attack:

The representations above are meant to convey that both a False Vision and a Physical Manifestation attack are taking place at the same time, to some extent or another. The brain is sensory-hacked so that the abductee may perceive themselves to be in a new location, and whatever they experience can seem physically real. At the same time, the abductee may incur physical injuries from a level of Physical attack, in partial physical manifestation. While the abductee perceives themself to be aboard a spaceship, and bruised by an alien, the fallen angel manifests physically enough to cause a bruise on the body of the abductee in the corresponding area. In fact, the abductee is in green reality, still located in the same hallway, though having a False Vision of being somewhere else.

An especially deceptive aspect of a False Visions combined with a degree of Physical Manifestation, is when the attack begins with a real-feeling False Vision of the abductee's actual location. For instance, the abductee may actually be in their bedroom, and the Vision begins with the fallen angel having them perceive their bedroom, in a way that seems completely physically real. The real-seeming Vision then includes the abductee being moved from their bedroom to a spaceship, and the travel out of the house to the spaceship, even being floated through a wall or out a window, while the experience continues to be so physically-real-seeming that it is indistinguishable from reality to the abductee. The effect is seamless and flawless, and can convince the abductee that the travel and the location they went to were physically real locations that exist in objective reality. However, without actual objective proof of this, nothing can be confirmed. The simplest explanation is that the abductee had a False Vision which felt completely real, as their brain, through which they perceive their senses, was under attack and being manipulated in it's signals by a fallen angel.

Abductees have reported being taken to underground military bases, a hollow earth, other planets, going there on spaceships with advanced propulsion and anti-gravity systems, underground secret railway systems, and going through portals, wormholes, teleportation, etc. sometimes with corresponding technology seen. Yet, there is no objective evidence that the abductee actually went anywhere by these methods the abductee saw. Even in cases in which the abductee was observed to be missing, it is not ruled out that the witness was also being affected by a fallen angel with a False Vision, so designed that they would not be able to see the abductee, even if the abductee was right in front of them. This is the interpretation I have of the several cases of abduction accounts I referenced prior; the abductee did not go anywhere but was prevented from being seen.

Also, even if there were in fact secret military underground bases in existence, and there was verifiable proof that this was a true fact in actual reality, this does not mean that any abductees have actually been to these places. There is a verifiable planet Mars, but that this place exists does not mean that any abductee has actually been taken to the planet Mars. The government may have top-secret advanced military aircraft, but that does not mean that an abductee has actually ridden on any such aircraft. Without verifiable proof, an equally valid explanation is that the abductee experienced a real-seeming False Vision which was deceptive, and intelligently designed to be deceptive by a fallen angel.

When the abductee sees supernatural occurrences during their experience, things that seems to defy the laws of physics, like passing through a wall, or severe injuries that would kill a person but have healed the next morning, technology that not only is unknown but in fact science has so-far concluded does something which is impossible (like a device that makes a wormhole), these are all indicators of a real-seeming False Vision experience.

Also, if the abductee sees other abductees, or military personnel, or humans that are real people who are living today, these could still just be part of a real-seeming False Vision, and is not conclusive proof that the abductee went anywhere, or saw actual other people. A particular John Doe might be a real person, but that an abductee saw John Doe during their abduction experience does not mean that John Doe was involved with the abductee's experience in any way. Some abductees report seeing "Jesus" during their experience, or seeing a dead spouse, yet in neither case was the actual person involved. Just as easily as a fallen angel can cause a False Vision of several aliens, so also can a fallen angel cause a False Vision of human beings, even ones who really exist. There are some documented cases of one abductee seeing another abductee in an experience, and meeting that very person later in their life. In this case it is entirely possible that the fallen angels simply knew that both people were abductees, as the abductions were being caused by these fallen angels, and incorporated this fact into a False Vision, given to one or both abductees. That the people met later in life (like a UFO Conference) could be a coincidence that was merely hoped for by the fallen angel, or it even could be that the abductee was influenced towards the decision to go to this event by the fallen angel.

Once the enormity of the abilities of deception that a fallen angel has at their disposal by use of these methods, sinks in, it becomes very clear just how little of the information gleaned from abductee reports can be assumed to serve as verifiable proof of what is taking place in objective reality. In abductee cases, usually the only thing that can really be accepted as true is that the person really had an "alien abduction experience". However, very little information can be gathered from the content of that experience. The abductee really did experience an event, but like one can't trust what a channeled demon says to a contactee to be true, one cannot trust what a fallen angel causes an abductee to experience in a False Vision to be true either. It is true that the abductee experienced something, and something truly traumatic, and can need all the understanding of someone who experienced a real trauma, because they have. (And the Bible always records Visions as actual events that happened to the person who experienced the Vision, even though it is specified that the experience was a Vision. The Bible also confirms these events can be truly traumatic, besides in Job 7, also see Dan 8:27 and 7:28.) Yet at the same time the information that can be gathered from the content of a False Vision experience cannot be trusted, as all of it is a purposely designed deception caused by a fallen angel, working in the dark army of Satan who is the father of lies.

In conclusion, Science and Modern Physics seems to allow for the miraculous and miracles, whether caused by God, Holy angels or fallen angels. For Christians, the Bible does establish the kinds of things that fallen angels can do. Taking the Bible as the authoritative Word of God, on faith, there really is no need to question that fallen angels have these abilities. The Bible says fallen angels have these abilities, both of whatever degree of physical effects, and causing False Visions and dreams. Bible-believing Christians should be able to accept that, whether modern science has caught up to the Truth of the Word of God, or not. But the hope with this piece is that you can understand that Science and the Bible do not conflict, as science actually allows for the miraculous to occur, as is recorded in the Bible and seen in miracles God still works today. And as also is seen in the false signs and wonders that happen today, caused by fallen angels. Theories in Science are always changing, in a progressive accumulation of knowledge: they are not truth. Where the Bible and science seem to contradict, I believe the Bible should always be deferred to as Correct and Truth, no matter what science teaches or scientists say.

I've touched on topics involved with big bang theory, quantum mechanics, black holes, worm holes, extra dimensions, and string theory. But I agree with what Russell Grigg, from CMI-Australia has to say on this:

"It has truly been said that Christians married in their thinking to today's science (e.g. big bang, ten dimensions, etc.) will be widowed tomorrow."
-Russell M. Grigg M.Sc. (Hons.), Creationist Chemist and Missionary www.creation.com CMI-Australia

That being said, I'm not entirely convinced about any of these theoretical science theories, and my intent here has not been to convince anyone of them. But rather, the aim of this was to use Modern Physics theories to show that science does not contradict or in any way disallow what that Bible teaches is true. The main point of doing this is to show that science does not preclude the existence of miracles of God and of holy angels, and also the false miraculous done by fallen angels. But rather I believe modern science actually completely allows for miracles, and for fallen angels, and their Biblically described abilities.

It is clear that the Bible says fallen angels can do things as are described in "alien abduction" accounts. There is nothing in modern science that contradicts or disproves what the Bible teaches about fallen angels and their abilities. Rather than prove this seemingly supernatural activity is impossible, science actually completely allows for all of this to be possible...

Modern physics shows that God created the universe to leave room for the miraculous to occur, without violating the laws of physics that He set up and maintains. Regarding "alien abduction" experiences, the explanation of fallen angels causing False Visions actually makes far more sense and violates known science and modern science theories far less than the biological extraterrestrial with advanced technology explanation.

In any case, God is infinitely dimensional, without any question, having created all dimensions and everything in them, and as we know, God, in His three persons, can do anything and is All-powerful.

A fallen angel is more powerful than a human. But Jesus Christ is the Son of God, fully God and fully man, and also infinitely dimensional. So Jesus Christ is more powerful than any fallen angel, and even more powerful than all fallen angels combined. This is just another way of looking at what we already know, that Jesus Christ is seated at the right hand of God, with all power, above every other power, principality, authority, above every angel, Holy or fallen.

Angels can only be in one place at once, as we see in Daniel 10. And angels were created by God, as Genesis says, "God created the heavens and the earth and all the host of them".

But Jesus Christ is the fullness of the Godhead in human form, and Jesus Christ said "before Abraham was, I AM", and John tells us "All things were made by him; and without him was not any thing made that was made", showing Jesus Christ's infinite dimensionality as the Son of God.

And the Bible tells us in Acts 4:10-12,
Be it known unto you all, and to all the people of Israel, that by the name of Jesus Christ of Nazareth, whom ye crucified, whom God raised from the dead, [even] by him doth this man stand here before you whole. This is the stone which was set at nought of you builders, which is become the head of the corner. Neither is there salvation in any other: for there is none other name under heaven given among men, whereby we must be saved.

<u>And we see this in abductions stopping in the name of Jesus Christ. Jesus Christ can and does help those who call out to Him for His help, and who have faith in Him and believe upon the power of His Name.</u>

So Jesus Christ is more powerful than fallen angels, in whatever form they take, one example being aliens, no matter how powerful they seem, Jesus Christ is more powerful.

And we also see this in that many other supernatural harassment and attacks stop in the name and authority of Jesus Christ. So Jesus Christ is more powerful than fallen angels, in whatever form they take, no matter how powerful they seem, Jesus Christ is more powerful. The Bible confirms this in every way, including symbolically.

Insectoid Aliens look like locusts, but the Bible tells us that the locusts will not harm those with the seal of God on their foreheads.

Rev 9:3-11 And there came out of the smoke **locusts** upon the earth: and unto them was given power, as the **scorpions** of the earth have power. And it was commanded them that they should not **hurt** the grass of the earth, neither any green thing, neither any tree; but **only those men which have not the seal of God in their foreheads**. And to them it was given that they should not kill them, but that they should be tormented five months: and their torment [was] as the **torment of a scorpion**, when he striketh a man. And in those days shall men seek death, and shall not find it; and shall desire to die, and death shall flee from them. And the shapes of **the locusts** [were] like unto horses prepared unto battle; and on their heads [were] as it were crowns like gold, and their faces [were] as the faces of men. And they had hair as the hair of women, and their teeth were as [the teeth] of lions. And they had breastplates, as it were breastplates of iron; and the sound of their wings [was] as the sound of chariots of many horses running to

battle. And they had tails **like unto scorpions**, and there were stings in their tails: and their power [was] to hurt men five months. **And they had a king over them, [which is] the angel of the bottomless pit,** whose name in the Hebrew tongue [is] Abaddon, but in the Greek tongue hath [his] name Apollyon.

Theses locusts are like scorpions, But Jesus tells us:

Luke 10:9 Behold, I **give unto you power to tread on serpents and scorpions**, and over all the power of the enemy: and nothing shall by any means hurt you.

Reptilian Aliens also look like serpents, but Jesus gives power to us to tread upon scorpions and serpents!

Also, Gray Aliens look like frogs.

Rev 16:13-14 And I saw three unclean **spirits like frogs** [come] out of the mouth of the dragon, and out of the mouth of the beast, and out of the mouth of the false prophet. For they are the spirits of devils, working miracles, [which] go forth unto the kings of the earth and of the whole world, to gather them to the battle of that great day of God Almighty.

Frogs	"Gray Aliens" are said to have
Large eyes, slit mouth, no nose	Large eyes, slit mouth, no nose
3-4 long webbed fingers	3-4 long webbed fingers
No external genitalia	No external genitalia
No hair	No hair
Ability to Absorb through skin	Ability to Absorb through skin
External reproductive means	External reproductive means

But Jesus tells us:

Rev 19:10-16,19-21
And I saw heaven opened, and behold a white horse; and he that sat upon him [was] called **Faithful and True**, and in righteousness he doth judge and make war. His eyes [were] as a flame of fire, and on his head [were] many crowns; and he had a name written, that no man knew, but he himself. And he [was] clothed with a vesture dipped in blood: and his name is called **The Word of God**. And the armies [which were] in heaven followed him upon white horses, clothed in fine linen, white and clean.
And out of his mouth goeth a sharp sword, that with it he should smite the nations: and he shall rule them with a rod of iron: and he treadeth the winepress of the fierceness and wrath of Almighty God. And he hath on [his] vesture and on his thigh a name written, **KING OF KINGS, AND LORD OF LORDS**.
And I saw the beast, and the kings of the earth, and their armies, gathered together to make war against him that sat on the horse, and against his army.
And the beast was taken, and with him the false prophet that wrought miracles before him, with which he deceived them that had received the mark of the beast, and them that worshipped his image. These both were cast alive into a lake of fire burning with brimstone. And the remnant were slain with the sword of him that sat upon the horse, which [sword] proceeded out of his mouth: and all the fowls were filled with their flesh."

Jesus Christ the Lord will destroy the enemy, Jesus Christ will win the battle. In all the forms of that the enemy takes, aliens or whatever else, the Bible tells us that all power over the enemy, to defeat the enemy, is in the hands of the Lord Jesus Christ. The victory belongs to the Lord Jesus Christ.

Resources:

My main site: www.ParadoxBrown.com
Which contains my other book, "A Modern Guide to Demons and Fallen Angels"
More information on fallen angels, demons, Nephilim, alien abduction, spiritual warfare and "aliens" in Bible prophecy can be found online at my website.

For online videos and DVDs on this topic see:

www.TheInvisibleBattle.com

www.AncientofDays.net

www.ChristianSymposium.com

Being myself a young earth creationist, for answers to science questions I would highly recommend:

www.Creation.com

Also check out Gary Bates' book on the alien phenomenon at:

www.AlienIntrusion.com

For help in stopping abductions and more information on abductions, book and DVD resources go to:

www.AlienResistance.com

www.CE4Research.com

And related, also see:
www.StopSleepParalysis.org

Alien abductions stop, and can be terminated as a life pattern, in the name and authority of Jesus Christ!

www.ingramcontent.com/pod-product-compliance
Lightning Source LLC
Chambersburg PA
CBHW030000050426
42451CB00006B/70